ANDREW MARVELL

T0364306

Modellen om Sonne-wijfers van Palm te leggen.

ANDREW MARVELL

by

M. C. BRADBROOK
Fellow of Girton College

and

M. G. LLOYD THOMAS
Fellow of Girton College

CAMBRIDGE
AT THE UNIVERSITY PRESS
1961

CAMBRIDGE UNIVERSITY PRESS

Cambridge, New York, Melbourne, Madrid, Cape Town, Singapore,
São Paulo, Delhi, Dubai, Tokyo, Mexico City

Cambridge University Press
The Edinburgh Building, Cambridge CB2 8RU, UK

Published in the United States of America by
Cambridge University Press, New York

www.cambridge.org
Information on this title: www.cambridge.org/9780521153638

First published 1940
Reprinted 1961
First paperback edition 2010

A catalogue record for this publication is available from the British Library

ISBN 978-0-521-04303-8 Hardback
ISBN 978-0-521-15363-8 Paperback

CONTENTS

The later Sidney, Marvel, Harrington,
Young Vane, and others who called Milton friend.
These moralists could act and comprehend. . . .

WORDSWORTH

PREFACE

THIS BOOK is intended as a critical study of Marvell, both as a representative of his age and as individually remarkable. His writings illuminate the development of the English language during one of its most crucial periods, when the emergence of modern prose style resulted in rapid changes both in structure and vocabulary. Such problems are touched upon here as they would present themselves to students of English literature and manners, and not as they confront the philologist. For the consideration of Marvell's language inevitably involves the larger questions of the social and cultural habits of the time. The way in which words were used is intelligible only by reference to the contemporary background of ideas—to those limiting and habitual categories and distinctions of which every age is least conscious, and which are so difficult to recapture once they have been replaced by others.

A tentative chronological scheme, which takes account of Marvell's known connections, has been adopted for some of the poetry which cannot definitely be dated: this is not contradicted by the development shown in such poems as are of ascertainable date.

Little of the biographical material is new, but some documents which are not widely known have been reprinted in part. The large number of quotations from Marvell's prose in Chapters IV and V are intended to give some material for independent judgment to those readers who have no access to the originals or to the rare reprints of his work.

No bibliography is included, as both the texts and the secondary material have been fully dealt with in the valuable work of M. Pierre Legouis, *André Marvell, poète, puritain, patriote* (Henri Didier and Oxford University Press, 1928). Our general indebtedness to M. Legouis will be evident. The text of the poems and letters is taken from H. M. Margoliouth's *Poems and Letters of Andrew Marvell*, 2 vols., Oxford University Press, 1927; the punctuation of the poems has in one or two instances been corrected in accordance with the 1681 Folio. The texts of *The Rehearsal Transpros'd*, both parts, are those of the second editions; the copy of the Second Part (1674) was kindly lent by Professor F. P. Wilson. For the rest of Marvell's prose the first editions have been used, but for the convenience of the reader the page references have been also given to Grosart's edition, *The Works of Andrew Marvell*, 4 vols., Fuller Worthies' Library, 1873-5. The Mock-Speech, of which there is no authoritative printed text, is given from British Museum MS. Add. 34,362.

The authors are indebted to Mr T. S. Eliot for leave to use material which has appeared in *The Criterion*, and to Professor Sir A. E. Richardson for the frontispiece.

M. C. B.

M. G. Ll. T.

CAMBRIDGE

June 1940

NOTE ON 1961 REPRINT

Apart from the correction of misprints, this is a reprint of the edition of 1940. For discussion arising from the interpretation of 'The Nymph Complaining for the death of her Faun', see E. S. Le Comte, *Modern Philology*, L (1952), 97–101; K. Williamson, *ibid*, LI (1954), 268–71; E. H. Emerson and Pierre Legouis, *Études Anglaises*, VIII (1955), 107–12; Leo Spitzer, *Modern Language Quarterly*, XIX (1958), 231–43; Don Cameron Allen, *Image and Meaning* (Baltimore, 1960), 93–114.

H. M. Margoliouth's edition was reprinted with some changes in 1951: some recent bibliographical information is to be found in Hugh Macdonald's edition of the Poems (Muses' Library, Routledge, 2nd ed., 1956).

I

'A MAN OF SINGULAR DESERT'

'Mr Marvile: a man whom both by report and the converse I have had with him, of singular desert for the
State to make use of: who also offers himself....'

Milton to Bradshaw, 21 February 1652/3.

ANDREW MARVELL's life and achievements were
of a sure and civilized kind which do not so readily
invite analysis as acceptance. During three centuries
he has fortified English tradition in very different ways.
From the time of his death till the beginning of the
nineteenth century he was remembered as a brave
and powerful fighter against intolerance, both political
and ecclesiastical: so Wordsworth remembered him.
Throughout the nineteenth century his reputation as
a poet increased, but it was that of a poet of nature
and simplicity; in the introduction to his edition of
the *Works* the delightfully impassioned Grosart describes him in terms which would have been more
suitably applied by the Poet Laureate to the Prince
Consort. In the twentieth century Marvell's reputation as a lyric poet has grown till his finest poems have
been compared, to their advantage, with Donne's,
but his other achievements are now generally forgotten. A critical examination of his total work
would seem to be due, and is the aim of this survey.
A consideration of his writing as a whole deepens the

effect and implications of the best: and some of his verse, and most of his prose, is not as well known as it deserves to be. A brief preliminary sketch of Marvell's career, the subject of the present chapter, is a necessary preliminary to such a survey.

The known facts of his life are few. He was born on 31 March 1621, at Winestead in Holderness, the son of an Anglican clergyman, Andrew Marvell (whose family came from Meldreth, near Cambridge), and of Anne Pease, a Yorkshire woman. In 1624, his father became 'Lecturer' of Holy Trinity Church, Hull, and Master of the Charterhouse. Marvell was educated at the Grammar School, Hull, and at Trinity College, Cambridge, where he was in residence from 1633 to 1640.[1] Here he published his first verses.

After going down he travelled for four years in Holland, France, Italy and Spain and acquired a knowledge of their languages. (Contemporaries rated his linguistic powers highly.) He had therefore left the country just about the time when the war broke out, and when he came back, his views seem to have been moderately Royalist, if they may be deduced from the elegy on Lord Hastings, and his poem prefixed to Richard Lovelace's *Lucasta*, both published in 1649. The attitude expressed in *An Horatian Ode upon Cromwel's Return from Ireland* (written presumably for the immediate occasion) indicates that he had by 1650 become a moderate Parliamentarian. Moreover, early in the next year, 1651, Marvell became tutor in foreign languages to the daughter of Lord Fairfax.

[1] As the Grammar School's Exhibitioner and College Scholar.

Fairfax had been a generous and moderate leader of the Parliamentary forces: but he retired from command upon a point of conscience. He had never advocated extreme measures, and was widely known to be merciful; he had refused to concur in the King's execution, and he headed the deputation which invited the return of Charles II, so that the family might be described as being politically of the centre.[1]

Marvell lived with the Fairfaxes for two years at Nunappleton House, in his own county of Yorkshire, and it has been presumed that here he wrote many of his lyrics. England was now almost peaceful after the Battle of Worcester; a reasonable majority at least could settle down to ordinary living.

To some it has seemed strange, and even reprehensible, that Marvell did not take more active part in the Civil War. But the issues were extremely involved, and many of the better men on either side were divided in allegiance and perplexed about their party. There is the further difficulty, with Marvell, of an absence of information about his doings.

For the crucial years 1644 (the date of his return to England) to 1650 there is no evidence at all of what he was about, and judgment must therefore be reserved.[2] His own words 'I think the Cause was too good

---

[1] There is a new biography by M. A. Gibb, *The Lord General* (Lindsay Drummond, 1938).

[2] His later connection with Sir George Downing, Cromwell's Scoutmaster-General, a passage in the *Calendar of State Papers Domestic*, 1671, p. 496, and some of the evidence collected by Prof. Tupper in the article cited in n. 1, p. 9, suggest as a possibility that Marvell was found useful for intelligence work by successive governments.

to have been fought for'[1] and some of the passages in
Upon Appleton House make it clear that he thought the
war brutal and avoidable, and that he thought more
of the soil of England than he did of either party. If
he were a trimmer it was in Halifax's sense:

> Our *Trimmer* is far from Idolatry in other things, in one
> thing only he cometh near it, his Country is in some
> degree his Idol; he doth not Worship the Sun, because
> 'tis not peculiar to us, it rambles about the World, and is
> less kind to us than others; but for the Earth of *England*,
> tho perhaps inferior to that of many places abroad, to
> him there is Divinity in it, and he would rather dye,
> than see a spire of *English* Grass trampled down by a
> Foreign Trespasser: He thinketh there are a great many
> of his mind, for all plants are apt to taste of the Soyl in
> which they grow, and we that grow here, have a Root
> that produceth in us a Stalk of English Juice, which is
> not to be changed by grafting or foreign infusion.[2]

Such words, had he lived to read them, might have
been welcome to the Marvell who wrote:

> Oh Thou, that dear and happy Isle
> The Garden of the World ere while,
> Thou *Paradise* of four Seas,
> Which *Heaven* planted us to please,
> But, to exclude the World, did guard
> With watry if not flaming Sword;
> What luckless Apple did we tast,
> To make us Mortal, and The Wast?

Marvell identified the country and the ruler as Halifax
was later to do in observing that

> ...when either of them undertake to act a part, it is like
> the crawling of Worms after they are cut in pieces, which

---

[1] Grosart, *Works*, Vol. III, p. 212.
[2] George, Marquis of Halifax, *Works*, ed. Raleigh (Oxford, 1912),
p. 97.

cannot be a lasting motion, the whole Creature not stirring at a time.

But a gradual conviction that the Parliamentary government was in fact best for the country seems to have led Marvell to attach himself more definitely to its members. At all events it is in 1652/3 that he emerges from his retired and elusive way of living into public life, for we find him in Milton's letter of 21 February offering himself for government service. He did not get the position at the time, but was appointed tutor to Cromwell's ward, William Dutton, who was living at Eton in the house of John Oxenbridge: to judge from a number of occasional complimentary poems written by Marvell at this time, he had friends engaged in foreign diplomacy. In 1657 he became Assistant in the office of the Foreign Secretary, the post for which Milton had recommended him, and a year later he was elected one of the two members of Parliament for Hull.

Marvell served in this capacity for twenty years, till the time of his death; but his literary activity, though equally continuous, was not equally un-modified. Hitherto he had written a few poems for official occasions, but had not published many of them. He now began to write his series of verse attacks upon the government policy and his satires of the royal family and the leaders of government, which were of course anonymous; but even so, it was a dangerous occupation.

In 1662 Marvell went to Holland, and stayed at the Hague in the house of Sir George Downing, the British Minister: the object of this visit is not known, but since Marvell speaks of being 'obliged' to go by some persons 'too potent for me to refuse', he was probably engaged in diplomacy. But he had also 'private affairs' there, and as Holland was the rallying place for Presbyterian exiles, his visit is open to interesting interpretation,[1] especially when it is remembered that L'Estrange later accused him of being the Secretary of the secret club of the Opposition, which met in coffee houses. He stayed abroad for ten months.

In 1663–5 Marvell travelled through Russia, Denmark and Sweden as Secretary to the Embassy of the Earl of Carlisle (Downing's brother-in-law).[2] He was absent about eighteen months.

During the last six years of his life he became famous as a pamphleteer. He defended the toleration of Dissent; on three occasions he intervened in controversy, and silenced his opponents. This was also a dangerous occupation, and his success made it no safer. Though the pamphlets were technically anonymous, their authorship was generally known.

Marvell had a reputation as a wit in the coffee houses, and about town, but he did not speak much

[1] See Margoliouth, *Letters to Hull*, Nos. 31–2: *Trinity House Letters*, Nos. 5–6. See also Appendix C for another interest of the journey. Marvell had many connections with Holland. Sir George Downing had represented Cromwell at the Hague, and continued to hold the same position under Charles. See John Beresford, *The Godfather of Downing Street* (Cobden-Sanderson, 1925), chapters 4–9.

[2] See Appendix B. A part of the contemporary account of the embassy was reprinted as a school text, *A Journey to Russia in 1663*, by G. Miège (A. and C. Black, 1926). There is also a popular version of the Russian part in Baroness Sophie Buxhoeveden's *A Cavalier in Muscovy* (Macmillan, 1932).

in the House. He is popularly but erroneously supposed to have been the last member to have drawn
his salary of six shillings and eightpence a day during
session time. There are several apocryphal stories of
his refusing huge bribes from the Crown to stop his
pamphleteering.

Marvell died on 16 August 1678,[1] and was buried
in St Giles-in-the-Fields. His earlier poems were
published in folio in 1681, but this volume contained
none of the political poems; the British Museum's
copy is unique in having *An Horatian Ode, The First
Anniversary of the Government under O. C.* and a frag-
ment of *A Poem upon the Death of O. C.* The first two
also occur in one other copy, but were cancelled from
the rest of the edition.

The textual history of Marvell's works is long and
complicated since they were almost all either anonymous or posthumous. In his lifetime he published
under his own name only a few occasional poems
in collections[2] and the Second Part of *The Rehearsal
Transpros'd.* This work was his first excursus into
pamphleteering, and defended toleration against
Samuel Parker, who had attacked it fiercely in three
separate books. Marvell published the first part of his
answer anonymously, and indeed without a licence:
it would have been suppressed had not Charles himself
been sufficiently amused by it to order the licenser,
L'Estrange, to give his *imprimatur.* But Marvell's life

---

[1] The date has been disputed: but the latest evidence favours it.
See an appendix to the article by Prof. F. S. Tupper cited in n. 1, p. 9.
[2] See Legouis, *André Marvell*, pp. 453–5.

B

was threatened by members of the opposite faction, and as a general defiance to threatening letter-writers he published the second part under his own name. All other pamphlets and the verse satires were anonymous, though many pamphlets were reprinted soon after his death with his name attached; and after the revolution of 1688 the satiric verse also came out in print.

A certain amount of evidence about his pamphlets may be obtained from his letters, where he privately acknowledges several of them: but the authenticity of many of the smaller pieces and of the verse satires has not been decided, and it seems impossible that the canon of his works should ever be definitive. Until the discovery of the folio now in the British Museum, the ascription to Marvell of *An Horatian Ode* itself rested only on the word of a very unreliable editor.

Marvell seems to have maintained an attitude usual in the earlier part of his century, that a gentleman wrote his poetry to amuse his private friends; though a hostile pamphleteer said that he attempted 'to live upon poetry',[1] there is no supporting evidence. He published only such work as had been occasioned by an immediate public situation; everything that he is chiefly remembered for to-day was 'found since his Death among his other Papers'.

The story of the publication of Marvell's poems in

[1] *A Letter from Amsterdam to a Friend in England* (1678). Reprinted in *Somers' Tracts*, ed. Walter Scott, 1812, vol. VIII, p. 88: '...make sure of Andrew; he's a shrewd man against popery, though for his religion you may place him, as Pasquin at Rome placed Henry the Eighth, betwixt Moses, the Messiah, and Mahomet, with this motto in his mouth, *Quo me vertam nescio*. It is well he is now transposed into politicks; they say he had much ado to live upon poetry.'

the folio of 1681 is very curious and has only re-
cently been brought to light by Prof. F. S. Tupper.[1]
As it is long and complicated, it has been summarized in an appendix; it may be mentioned here
that Prof. Tupper has revealed the identity of 'Mary
Marvell' who signed the Note 'To the Reader'; she
was Mary Palmer, Marvell's housekeeper, and had
neither legal nor moral right to assume his name; her
purpose in assuming it was mercenary, as the earliest
editors of Marvell had stated on the authority of
his family. Her publication of the poems was however
the only attempt made to produce manuscript
material: copies remained at Hull, but Marvell's
family seem to have taken but little care to preserve
them.[2]

It has sometimes been lamented that Marvell
stopped writing lyric poetry when he began to serve
the State and thereafter wrote little poetry of any
kind. But there are no grounds for assuming that all
his lyrics belong to the Commonwealth period: the
religious and 'philosophic' poems in particular might
be put later; there is neither external nor direct in-
ternal evidence of their date.

[1] See F. S. Tupper, 'Mary Palmer, alias Mrs Andrew Marvell',
Publications of the Modern Language Association of America, June 1938
(vol. LIII, No. 2). Summarized in Appendix A.

[2] Captain Edward Thompson, who edited an edition of Marvell in
1776, incorporated the contents of two MSS. belonging to Marvell's
family, but including much that was not by him. The MSS. were
afterwards lost and it is believed Thompson destroyed them. (See
Margoliouth, *Poems*, pp. 212–14.) It was he who first reprinted *An
Horatian Ode*, and printed for the first time the end of *A Poem upon the
Death of O. C.* (ll. 185–234) which is missing in the British Museum's
folio.

It is understandable that he should feel a com-
pulsion to work for the State after the Restoration,
when he had refrained from fighting in the Civil War.
He had accepted Charles while Charles was king, he
had also come to accept the 'forced Pow'r' of Cromwell after Charles' execution: and when the Stuarts
were restored he accepted the Stuarts. To make the
best of whatever government was established was not
a capitulation: however much he personally disliked
the Restoration, the Cause would still remain too
good to be fought for. But when the government of
the country was jeopardized by irresponsible and self-
seeking rulers, the Cause demanded that he should do
his best to uphold the principles of right administra-
tion within the framework of the monarchy. It was
not a question of fighting for rival parties representing
different systems, but of maintaining standards of
integrity which should have been the property of
any system. The Cause was not political but moral.
Marvell attacked Charles' conduct, but he also upheld
the monarchy as an institution; and he attacked individual clerics but not the Church. The attitude was
not uncommon, perhaps, in a century which held
rebellion to be as the sin of witchcraft,[1] and when
religion was so much more important than politics
that it was their acknowledged basis. But the specifically political evils which followed the Restoration
were such that no man who had feelings stronger than
the merely political for constitutional government,
but who disapproved of settling things by the sword,

[1] See *Works*, ed. Grosart, vol. III, p. 87.

could live without being affected by, and involved in them.

The very language had coarsened and stiffened to an almost unbelievable extent. The poets themselves,—such as Otway and Dryden—judging from their adaptations of Shakespeare, appear to have had no greater sense of his poetry than of his construction. Milton, in enforced retirement, could ignore the rest of the world and write in his own particular idiom: the poetry of Rochester shows what effect the main tendency of the age could have upon a mind to which it was not congenial. The intellectual and literary climates must have been equally withering to Marvell: and to set the Nettleton against the Hollis portrait might serve as a demonstration of the effects of the Restoration upon their subject.

The few authentic stories and speeches which survive from this period show as paradoxical a portrait as could be imagined. Marvell had at times a fiery temper and the tongue of a bargee. Samuel Parker taunts him with his education among 'Boat-Swains and Cabin Boys', from whom he learned his language. His prose is hardly ever obscene; but in his verse he could speak with the unpremeditated fervour of the uneducated: and one story, related by Thompson, shows him tripping into the gutter the clerical enemy who had censored his language with a remark much more vigorous than decent.[1]

---

[1] Marvell's remark was 'Lye there for the son of a whore'. When reprimanded by the Bishop, he proved from Parker's works that Parker had in one place said he was 'a true son of his mother,

He was also once involved in a quarrel in the House of Commons, his friend Sir Philip Harcourt and he exchanging blows wherein 'Marvell flung about three or four times with his hat, and then gave Harcourt a box on the ears'; and his reply to the Speaker's reprimand was distinctly insubordinate:

> *Mr Marvell.* What passed was through great acquaintance and familiarity between us. He never gave him an affront nor intended him any. But the Speaker cast a severe reflection upon him yesterday when he was out of the House: and he hopes that, as the Speaker keep us in order, he will keep himself in order for the future.[1]

A scandalized member proposed to send Marvell to the Tower for this remark: but when Harcourt had substantiated his account, and Marvell had offered to 'sacrifice himself to the judgment of the House', it passed off.[2]

On an earlier occasion, Marvell's playful demonstration with a pistol had embroiled the suite of the Earl of Carlisle in a free fight with some German waggoners.[3]

the church of England', and in another that 'The church of England has spawned two bastards, the Presbyterians and the Congregationals'; and he was therefore justified in his use of the phrase.

[1] Anchitell Grey, *Debates* (1769), vol. IV, p. 329.

[2] *The Diary of John Milward*, 1666–8, ed. C. Robbins (Cambridge, 1938), records several speeches by Marvell; and the author of *A Common-Place-Book out of the Rehearsal Transpros'd* says, p. 12: 'He, like the *Humorous Lieutenant*, was taken up in great and important affairs of the State: *the Parliament may sit in* February, and then the Good old Cause and *The Work of all the Faithful* in the land require his Counsel in *Cabals*, and his Speeches in Publick, as the most sufficient *Statesman* and exact *Orator* that their Party does afford.'

[3] See Appendix B.

Yet on a general issue Marvell shows none of the passions common to his personal quarrels and to those verse satires on the private lives of the men supposed to administer the country. In the age when Monmouth had Sir John Coventry's nose slit, and Dryden was beaten by the followers of a Duke, it was necessary for a gentleman to be something of a ruffian: but the necessity was confined to those who were great enough to afford it.

The paradoxical nature of this composite portrait comes out as one observes that with his hastiness of temper Marvell combined a moderation in matters of belief as rare among his own party as among his enemies. He pleaded for toleration, but remained a monarchist, whilst being acutely aware of the character of Charles and the majority of his episcopal bench. The very speech for which Mr Speaker had cast 'a severe reflection' upon him protests the right of Charles and the unpopular James to their own religious opinions: it attacks the self-seeking of the clerics, but remains sober on the main issue.

Whatever prince God gives us, we must trust him. Let us not in prevention of future things so remote, take that immoderate care in this bill.[1] Sufficient unto the day is the evil thereof.... He desires that, during the king's reign, we may apply ourselves to preserve the Protestant Religion, not only in the profession of it, but that we may live up to it, in morality and virtue of religion and then you establish men against the temptations of Popery and a prince that may be popishly

[1] A bill 'for securing the Protestant Religion by educating the children of the Royal Family therein', directed against James Duke of York.

inclined. If we do not practice upon ourselves, all these Oaths and Tests are of no use: they are but phantoms.[1]

A man who could respect James when he 'changed for conscience sake' to Catholicism, and who could speak of trusting Charles as men 'might and ought to have trusted' his father, shows a soundness of judgment too undeviating to be merely imposed and assumed. The same kind of judgment can be found again and again in his letters, and, in general, impartiality presides in his pamphlets. The violence which apparently conflicts with it may be explained perhaps as the inevitable relief and compensation, the instinctive safety valve for public and personal feelings which were bound to be outraged by the conduct of affairs and by the characters of those who conducted them: and the sanity and generosity of his judgment upon matters of principle could not have survived had he not sometimes shown 'a very, very pajock'.

Aubrey, who was a friend of Marvell, has left the only known contemporary sketch of him:

He was a great master of the Latin tongue; an excellent poet in Latin or English: for Latin verses there was no man could come into competition with him.... He was of a middling stature, pretty strong sett, roundish faced, cherry-cheek't, hazell eie, browne haire. He was in his conversation very modest, and of very few words: and though he loved wine he would never drinke hard in company, and was wont to say that, *he would not play the good-fellow in any man's company in whose hands he would not trust his life*...He kept bottles of wine at his lodgeing, and

[1] See Grey's *Debates*, vol. IV, pp. 321–5.

many times he would drinke liberally by himselfe to re-
fresh his spirits, and exalt his muse. . . . James Harrington,
esq. (auctor *Oceanae*), was his intimate friend. John
Pell, D.D., was one of his acquaintance. He had not a
generall acquaintance.[1]

Apart from a few notes on his birth, education and
date of death, Aubrey has little else to say. Beyond
Aubrey, there are only the scantiest occasional references, many by men prejudiced against Marvell.[2]
From Aubrey alone we have an account corresponding
with the works: modesty, vivacity, reserve. Marvell's
choice of friends is perhaps more revealing than anything else: Milton, Harrington the political philo-
sopher, Pell the mathematical scholar, Richard Lovelace, Richard Baxter, John Owen, John Hales of
Eton.

[1] *Brief Lives*, ed. Clark, vol. II, pp. 53–4.
[2] The chief exception is a MS. collection of poems in the autograph
of Will Popple, Marvell's nephew (B.M. Add. 8,888). This contains,
besides an epitaph for Marvell, a purely formal kind (*vide infra*,
p. 140), a verse translation of part of Horace, *Car*. lib. 3, ode 3, headed
The Character of a Virtuous Statesman. The translation is presumably
Popple's and it would certainly apply to Marvell:

> The upright Man whom sense of Duty guides,
> Thorow the Fluctuating Waves of State,
> Steers on his Steady Course.
> He stems the Torrents of opposing Tides,
> He bears up midst the Traverses of Fate,
> Nothing his Rectitude of Mind can warp or force.
> The furious Heats of Popular Zeal,
> Rais'd on mistaken views of Common Weal,
> The threat'ning Frowns of angry Kings,
> Urging Obedience in unlawfull things;
> Shake not his Virtues Adamantine Rock,
> But tho' ev'n Nature's Machin be unfixt,
> Though Heav'n and Earth be in Confusion mixt;
> He then undaunted Stands and does abide the Shock.

The friendship with Milton is the longest and the one of which we have most record: it lasted from before 1653 till Milton's death in 1674. It is known from Marvell's and Milton's letters, from the offices they held under Cromwell, from Philips' assertion that Marvell collected a party for Milton in the House when he was arrested after the Restoration, and presented the petition praying for a reduction of his prison fees. It is also recorded by Aubrey in his life of Milton, and by the different writers who attacked Marvell for writing *The Rehearsal Transpros'd*. It is further attested by Marvell's defence of Milton in the second part of *The Rehearsal Transpros'd* and the verses written for the second edition of *Paradise Lost*,—verses which touch gently on his blindness (which had been brutally handled by the pamphleteers), and defend his blank verse:

> At once delight and horrour on us seize,
> Thou singst with so much gravity and ease;
> And above humane flight dost soar aloft,
> With Plume so strong, so equal, and so soft.[1]

Milton died in the same year as this second edition appeared.

From this poem we also gather that Marvell was no admirer of Dryden, and in *The Epistle to the Whigs* (1682) and the preface to *Religio Laici* (1682) Dryden glances at Marvell. In the preface he says:

Martin Mar-prelate (the *Marvel* of those times) was the first Presbyterian Scribler who sanctify'd Libels and Scurrility to the use of the Good Old Cause.

[1] *On Mr Milton's Paradise lost*, ll. 35–8.

It may therefore not have been entirely accidental that Marvell chose as the basis of his first pamphlet a drama satirizing Dryden; there seems to have been no more love lost between the first Mr Bayes and himself than the second.

It is worth noting that the second Mr Bayes, Samuel Parker, was a follower of Hobbes in matters of literary style, as well as in other matters. He led the attack upon the Cambridge Platonists, who

> put us off with nothing but rampant metaphors and Pompous Allegories and other splendid but empty schemes of speech...to Discourse of the Natures of Things in Metaphor and Allegory is nothing else but to sport or trifle with empty words, because these Schems do not express the Natures of Things but only their Similitude and Resemblances.[1]

and he even advocated an Act of Parliament 'to abridge the use of fulsom and lushious Metaphors'.[2]

Marvell would not have accepted Parker's or the Royal Society's receipt for writing prose: he used a wide vocabulary, archaisms, neologisms, Gallicisms, as it suited him, and he avoided 'fulsom and lushious Metaphors' so little that his enthusiastic language was one of the regular points of attack.

He remarked, according to Aubrey, 'that the earle of Rochester was the only man in England that had the true veine of satyre'.[3] Rochester reciprocated this goodwill in his poem on Tunbridge Wells:

---

[1] *A Free and Impartial Censure of the Platonick Philosophy* (1666), p. 73.
[2] *Discourse of Ecclesiastical Policy* (1670), p. 76.
[3] *Brief Lives*, ed. cit. vol. II, pp. 54, 304.

> Listening, I found the Cobb of all the Rabble,
> Was pert Bayes, with Importance comfortable;
> He being rais'd to an Arch-deaconry,
> By trampling on Religious Liberty;
> Was grown so fat and looked so big and jolly,
> Not being disturbed with care and melancholy,
> Tho' *Marvel* has enough expos'd his folly.[1]

To have been the friend of Milton, hailed a wit by Rochester, disliked by Dryden, and known to scarcely anyone was something of a feat. Marvell was sufficiently in sympathy with the Restoration temper to be looked upon as a coffee-house wit, and to satirize with the authority of an insider: he was also sufficiently a Puritan to be satirized in his turn by Restoration clergy and Restoration actors, such as Hickeringill and Richard Leigh. From these virulent but stupid pamphlets against him, a few additional facts and hints about his life and habits may be gleaned.

Richard Leigh in *The Transproser Rehears'd* gives a scornful description of a party of *virtuosi* sitting in a coffee house enjoying *The Rehearsal Transpros'd*:

And now one sinks the *Dutch* in a dish of Coffee, and another beheading the clean Pipes, prognosticates the fate of *De Wit* and *Van Putten*, a third blows up a *Fire-ship* with a provident *Whiff* of Tobacco, and a fourth pouring a flood of Rheume upon the floor, opens the *Hollanders* Sluces.

The same writer makes most bitter personal attacks upon Marvell and Milton: he quotes 'Hail holy light, offspring of Heav'n first-born' at some length ('the odds betwixt a Blank Verse Poet and a *Transproser*

---

[1] *Poems on Affairs of State* (1697), p. 220. His 'comfortable Importance' was Marvell's nickname for Parker's mistress.

is not great') and spends a page or two jeering at the style and at Milton's blindness. He also observes that Marvell would be 'glad to lick up his spittle' (i.e. Milton's), and says he has taken all his essay on free printing from the *Areopagitica*. After professing great disgust at the 'filthiness' of Milton's divorce pamphlets, he goes on to accuse both of them of homosexuality, and Marvell of impotence:

> O marvellous fate! O fate full of marvel!
> That *Nol's Latin pay* two *clerks* should deserve ill!
> Hiring a *Gelding*, and *Milton* the *Stallion*;
> His *Latin* was gelt and turn'd pure *Italian*.

This is the level upon which a good deal of the fight is conducted.

The author of *S'too Him, Bayes*, is extremely supercilious and writes about Marvell's poverty, insinuating that he would be glad of a good dinner, and that he was paid for writing by poor Dissenters who took up collections at their conventicles. (This is repeated in other pamphlets.)

> He wanted food and linen: so he took
> Toleration for his Seamstress and his Cook.

And then he cries out like *King Harry* in *Shakespeare*, *My conscience! My conscience!* He has not the *Conscience* to see himself want: and 'tis pity he should.[1]

This writer also affects to take Marvell for a Jesuit.

In *Gregory Father Greybeard*, Marvell's fashionable

---

[1] P. 62. The verse is a parody of two lines in Cleveland's *Rebel Scot* and glances at Marvell's adaptation, *The Loyall Scot*. For Marvell's poverty see *S'too Him, Bayes*, pp. 62, 86, 124; *Gregory Father Greybeard*, pp. 17, 263–73 (both of which appeared in 1673); *A Love Letter to the Author of the Rehearsall Transpros'd*, ll. 145–254.

manners are stressed, in particular his use of Gallicisms like *tuant*, *remark*, *repartee*: he is called *Virtuoso*, *Ingenioso*, *Politico*. His wearing of a fashionable full-bottomed wig is reproached as an equal crime.[1] The following passage suggests some personal grounds for dislike, since the writer, Hickeringill, was a clergyman who rather prided himself on his wit:

> Have you never a little Clergy-man here, for a Gentle-man to play with? never a *Droll*, or *boon* companion with a *Cassock* on? that forgetting his *serious office*, will *make* a Gentleman *merry*, & rather than fail, with a Joque upon Scriptures make a *little Play?* that I may pass upon him once or twice: and with a *lucky hit*, (or as he phrases it, p. 312. with an unlucky Repartee,) jear the Parson, make him a scorn, a tail and contempt to the people.[2]

On the other hand Hickeringill also describes Marvell as being in the pay of the Dissenters, and compares him with Hugh Peters, the preacher who was hanged, drawn, and quartered as a regicide. Hugh Peters is the original 'Father Greybeard', and on p. 9 of the pamphlet it is suggested that he was one of the actual executioners of Charles I. Hickeringill writes parodies of one of Peters' sermons and of a speech by Marvell in the House, using the Hudibrastic metre. He too, like Parker, objects violently to long sermons and prayers, or anything savouring of eloquence; and in general he takes up the attitude of the plain blunt man, who writes 'not to instruct my Governours and tutour

---

[1] For the first see *Gregory Father Greybeard*, p. 30. For the second, *ibid.* pp. 35, 138, 172, 173, 207, etc. Marvell's wig seems to exasperate Hickeringill more than anything else. In the Hollis and Nettleton portraits he wears his own hair: in the one prefixed to the poems of 1681, adapted from the Nettleton portrait, he has a flowing curly wig.

[2] P. 202.

Kings, I thank God, I was never such a conceited thing nor so lost to all modesty and sense of humility' (p. 322), but to rebuke the pretensions of these political *virtuosi*.

Other pamphleteers repeat this charge of the Puritan masquerading as a town wit.[1] Poverty and fashionable manners, friendship with Dissenters and frequenting of coffee houses combine so strangely that it may be supposed that even caricature would not employ them without some foundation. The jibe about coffee houses may of course refer only to Marvell's membership of the Rota Club, and to the secret societies which were supposed to be modelled on it during the Restoration period:

> Certainly not every man that hath set his foot in Holland and Venice, or read Baxter's *Holy Commonwealth* and Harrington's *Oceana*, and made a speech once in the Rota, is statesman complete enough for such an undertaking.[2]

The Rota, a kind of model Parliament, met at Miles' coffee house in 1659. It discussed philosophy and politics: and the method of election seems to have been taken over by Milton in *A Ready and Easy Way to Establish a Free Commonwealth*. The Rota had '(very formally) a *balloting-box*, and balloted how things should be caried, by way of tentamens'.[3] The leader was James Harrington. It was esteemed such a centre of wit that the Parliamentary debates were but flat in

---

[1] *A Common-Place-Book out of the Rehearsal Transpros'd*, pp. 21–2 and *A Love Letter to the Author of The Rehearsall Transpros'd*, a verse satire, which we know only from Legouis, *André Marvell*, pp. 459–60.

[2] *The Transproser Rehears'd*, p. 147.

[3] Aubrey, *Brief Lives*, ed. cit. vol. 1, p. 290.

comparison, and it was not very favourably seen. The Rota probably encouraged the new member of Parliament in that interest in minutiae of constitutional procedure, which comes out in his satires, as well as giving him his apprenticeship to coffee-house conversations. Yet in spite of his reputation as virtuoso, his journey to Russia, his correspondent in Persia, Marvell remained soberly attached to his birthplace and to his common duties in the House. It is his long painstaking despatches to the burgesses of Hull which form the bulk of the *Letters*; and in these, the only two interests which are allowed are those of the Commons' business, and the business of the town. Nor does the question of the Dutch war engage Marvell more deeply than the problem of the local charter. From the whole tone of the letters, it is plain that Marvell did not have to limit himself deliberately in order to take the proper measure of the town affairs: his interests were cosmopolitan, but his feelings were not only those of a patriot but of a solidly local patriot into the bargain; and if he were ready to risk his ears in the cause of right government he was called upon to forgo his dinner in the service of Hull:

Really the businesse of the house hath been of late so earnest daily and so long, that I have not had the time and scarse vigour left me by night to write to you And to day because I would not omit any longer I lose my dinner to make sure of this Letter.[1]

Hull was probably not interested in his literary activities, but it recognized the tie by presents of Yorkshire ale in his lifetime and by voting the money

[1] Margoliouth, *Letters to Hull*, No. 68.

for a large and respectable tombstone after his death. At the very end of his life, his local attachments remained so much stronger than his public spirit as to lead him into circumventing the law.[1] The combination of subtlety and straightforwardness which was Marvell's strength as a writer reflects similar qualities in his ordinary life—the range of his general connections together with the undeviating simplicity of his devotion to the town where he was brought up. The Yorkshire countryside which his best poetry conserves, in agreement with it, is both delicate and austere. Each possesses a clarity which deepens and enriches and at the same time defines its colours; each has an unimpoverished frugality which is a source and mark of tenacious vigour. 'All that sternness amid charm, All that sweetness amid strength'.

Marvell was particularly dependent upon circumstances. He needed a suitable 'climate of opinion', a generous co-operation of environment and of mood. This sensitiveness to the social tone and temper can be seen most clearly in his political poems, where one particular juncture enables him to write, another makes writing almost impossible. The weakness of his later writings is that, for all their wit, they are so far inseparable from the particular events which stimulated them, that they are too occasional to be of permanent interest. He was exasperated, pricked by contemporary events and could not escape from them.[2]

[1] See Appendix A.
[2] He recognized his own weakness. 'I am so subject to be particular', he writes to Harley (Margoliouth, *Misc. Letters*, No. 27).

C

It was the same sensitiveness which made possible, at the right moment, his best lyric.

At Nunappleton he was probably more free (in the sense of being more detached) than at any other time in his life: and the particular moments, the particular things, in his environment, which moved him were those that gave rise to *Upon Appleton House* and *The Garden*. He was in the service of a man after his own heart, and the great local leader; Fairfax was, in life, as Marvell so often describes him, incurably modest and shy; a lover of solitude, and, moreover, a lover of books and an antiquary, in whose library Marvell could find amongst other treasures a MS. of Chaucer; a poet even, though one of extreme *naïveté*. One of his poems, *The Solitude*, adapted from the French of Saint-Amant (perhaps at Marvell's suggestion) seems also to recall *Upon Appleton House*.[1] The General is describing the river Denton:

> Sometimes so cleare and so serene
> It seems as 'twere a looking glass,
> And to our views preventing seem
> As heavens beneath the water was.
> The sun in it's so clearly seene
> That, contemplating this bright sight,
> As 'twas a doubt whether itt had beene
> Himself or image gave the light,
> At first appearing to our eyes,
> As if he had fal'n from the skyes.[2]

Quoted by M. A. Gibb, *op. cit.* p. 287; from MS. Fairfax 40 in the Bodleian, a collection of the General's poems with 'innumerable interpolations and corrections showing the hours of labour lavished on it by the author'. They are touching in their painstaking badness.

[2] Cf. *Upon Appleton House*, ll. 635–40. In line 71 Marvell is making polite reference to one of Fairfax's pieces.

It was as the result of those years of uniquely peaceful and agreeable life, in his own country, and in such a setting of learning, piety and rural privacy, that Marvell seems to have produced his best work; the particular animating circumstances bore, not lively *vers d'occasion*, but genuine poetry.[1]

[1] Mildmay Fane, Earl of Westmorland, and Fairfax's brother-in-law, was closer to Marvell as a poet. In *To Retiredness* (*Otia Sacra*, 1648) there are some striking parallels with *The Garden*. Fane describes how in his garden he 'as in a Trick' has all the pleasures of 'Riches and Honors', and how in his 'Contemplation' he is 'taught Thankfulness from trees':

> Here, is no other Case in Law,
> But what the *Sun-burnt* Hat of Straw,
> With crooked Sickle reaps and bindes...

Here his only War is the rivalry of the Birds and he '[though unseen must judg the Song'. He 'huggs his Quiet...':

> And deem in doing so, I've all
> I can True Conversation call:
> For so my Thoughts by this retreat
> Grow stronger, like contracted heat.   pp. 172–174.

Finally, whether he reads in 'Natures Book' or in another, he learns in retiredness to 'look to heaven' and 'ravish into Mysterie'.

The poem has been reprinted by L. Birkett Marshall, *Rare Poems of the Seventeenth Century* (Cambridge, 1936).

Another poem, *Anglia Hortus*, seems to foreshadow *Upon Appleton House*, XXXVI–XLVI:

> The Garden of the world, wherein the Rose
> In chief Commanded, did this doubt propose
> To be resolv'd in; Whether sense to prise
> For umpire to Create it Paradise:
> One led by th' Ear of Philomel tels tales,
> And straightway cal'st the land of Nightingales;
> An Other sharper sighted, ravish'd, cryes,
> O that I could be turn'd now all to eyes!
> A Third receiv'd such raptures from the tast
> Of various dainty fruits, that it surpast;
> A Fourth was caught (not with perfume) commends
> The Indian Clime, but what here Nature lends;
> Last, if you would Sattins or Velvets touch,
> For soft and smooth, Leaves can afford you such.
>> And thus dispos'd, whilst every Sense admires,
>> 'Tis sensless t'plant 'mongst Roses, Thistles, Briars.

(*Otia Sacra*, 1648, p. 133.)

II

THE CRITIC AND THE SWAIN

MARVELL'S poetry varies in the degree of its simplicity; but, at its simplest, it is not easy. He has several styles, but all of them rely, in ways more and less implicit, upon evanescent shades of meaning in a rapidly changing vocabulary, and upon those larger categories of thought, which are not at first sight very obvious to the reader of the present day. It is more usual to read him incompletely than to misread him, but his fine workmanship demands and repays a close analysis.

The following chapters attempt such an analysis of his poetry. It depends upon the finer shades of seventeenth-century vocabulary and so far it involves a consideration of the language; it depends also upon social attitudes and habits of thought and so far involves cultural history.

As regards language Marvell's writing covers an important transitional period, in which modern prose style emerged to meet the need of scientists; but emerged from a conflict in which Ciceronianism and Anti-Ciceronianism, the prescriptions of the philosophers and of the Royal Society, struggled together. In poetry there was almost another Civil War; and the 'reformers of our numbers', Denham and Waller, were put into a position which posterity has not ratified; the reputation of Cowley also resulted from the linguistic conflict and the course of his writings illustrates it. Marvell was by profession a linguist; his speeches for the Ambassador,[1] and his later pamphlets show a professional interest in words. Most of his poetry, however, belongs to the period between 1645 and 1660; it has a vocabulary not yet subjected to the 'dictionary' methods of Seth Ward and his Oxford friends, or the mathematical ideals of Hartlib and Wilkins:[2] it has the fluidity of Shakespeare's English, rather than those virtues of limitation and clarity which are associated with Dryden.

The new science and the new prose were at one. The same people attacked Platonism in philosophy, Hermeticism in science and 'pulpit eloquence'. Marvell's opponent Samuel Parker was active in all these fields. His theory of language is that it is purely a tool of science:[3]

> The use of Words is not to explain the Natures of Things, but only to stand as marks and signs in their stead, as Arithmetical figures are only notes of Numbers.[4]

The Cambridge Platonists are condemned on the score of their language:

> ...Though a huge lushious stile may relish sweet

[1] See Appendix A.

[2] Samuel Hartlib, *Common Writing* (1647); John Wilkins, *Ecclesiastes* (1646); *Essay towards a Real Character* (1668). See Otto Funke, *Zum Weltsprachenproblem in England im 17. Jahrhundert* (Anglistische Forschungen, Heft 69: Heidelberg, 1929).

[3] See the articles by Richard Jones, in *Pub. Mod. Lang. Ass. Amer.* vol. XLV, p. 977; *Jour. Eng. and Ger. Phil.* vol. XXX, p. 188, vol. XXXI, p. 315.

[4] *A Free and Impartial Censure of the Platonick Philosophy* (1666), p. 61.

to childish and liquorish Fancies, yet it rather loaths and nauceats a discreet understanding then forms and nourishes it.[1]

Such a theory would be incompatible with the practice of Marvell, some of whose poems (e.g. *Mourning* and *Daphnis and Chloe*) are entirely composed of strings of similes.

But the temper of the 1640's and 1650's was different. Then Fleckno (who in spite of Marvell's ridicule was fairly representative) could write:

Where have you for that which we call Rhetoricke, Eloquence and high Expression, a Language excelling ours? or that speaks more by Figure and Metaphor (the mayne ornaments of speech and the subtility of a Language) he being sayd to speak simply, whose words enfold not a double sense and meaning?[2]

The period of the Civil War and Commonwealth was one in which there were no great literary figures. Milton was doing government work: Herbert was dead: some of the works of great figures of the last generation, such as Jonson and Donne, were being published for the first time, but Waller, Cowley, Cleveland, Davenant were the poets of the day. It was a dull time; most writing was both elaborate and exhausted; in wartime, men's interests were elsewhere. While at Chicksands Dorothy Osborne read interminable French romances, at Nottingham Lucy Hutchinson read godly tracts.

In this world Marvell made his literary *début*. The elegies on Hastings and Villiers, the poems on Love-

[1] *Ibid.* p. 74.
[2] Richard Fleckno, *Miscellania* (1653), p. 102.

lace and Fleckno, can all be dated *c.* 1648–9; and it is probable that to this period belong *The Match, Mourning, Daphnis and Chloe, The Gallery* and *The unfortunate Lover.* These are all poems of the fashionable world, the compliments or scandal of a coterie. They all have a tinge of irony directed against the fashionable world; some are completely ironic. It is in these poems that Marvell is most modishly a 'metaphysical poet'. They are ingenious, complicated and almost entirely dependent on the flow of 'similitudes and resemblances'. *The Gallery* and *The unfortunate Lover* are composed of a series of emblematic pictures.[1] They are done in a series of heraldic cartoons, some of them fine enough; though the queer, semi-satiric hyperbole of *The unfortunate Lover* has been accepted as pure Clevelandism. This strictly emblematic lover—'In a Field *Sable* a Lover *Gules*'—from the very absurdity of his postures gains a certain power; everything that happens to him is savage and primitive, but the idea of creating him at all is sophisticated; and there is a genuine clash between the vigour of the language (e.g. the verbs 'split', 'roar', 'hurl'd', 'cuffing', 'grapple', 'torn') and the heraldic stiffness of the design. The 'masque of quarrelling Elements' is the only purely artificial scene in all Marvell's poetry.[2]

---

[1] *The unfortunate Lover* in particular recalls the series of emblems showing the lover's torments in Otto van Veen's *Amorum Emblemata* (Antwerp, 1608) and Crispin de Passe's *Thronus Cupidinis* (1618). See the technical work of Professor Mario Praz, *Studies in Seventeenth Century Imagery* (Warburg Institute, 1939).

[2] It has been suggested to us by Miss Syfret that the poem is a political allegory and that 'Th' unfortunate and abject Heir' who rules only 'in Story' is Charles Prince of Wales, cast away in the

In *The Fair Singer* there is a single metaphor running through the poem, that of the 'sweet enemy'. The mood is certainly gallant but somehow rather coolly egotistical:

> To make a final conquest of all me....
> But how should I avoid to be her Slave....
> And all my Forces needs must be undone....

There is really more about the great impression the lady was fortunate enough to make than about the lady herself:[1] the same is true of *The Gallery*, save in the last and natural picture of the 'tender Shepherdess' which she was at first.

In all these poems the conceits are too detached and over-elaborated, but in one or two others there is a single flash of illumination which holds the poem together. In *Daphnis and Chloe* and *Mourning*, which are frankly ironic, it is Nature, the Nature of the pastorals, which supplies the positive standards by which the courtly lovers are criticized. In each poem, at that point where the satiric intention reveals itself, there is a clear direct metaphor of natural beauty, which recalls to the mind something more satisfying and more lovely than is known in this world of polite society.

In *Daphnis and Chloe*, after the cruel fair has been betrayed by the grief of parting into kindness,

---

Scilly Isles after the failure of the Royalist cause in the West in 1646. The mother of verse two would then be England, the Rock religious controversy, and the cormorants Grenville and Goring.

[1] This poem is perhaps modelled on Lovelace's *To Gratiana Singing and Dancing*. There is also a reminiscence of Lovelace in *The unfortunate Lover* (see note to l. 57 in Margoliouth's edition).

> At that *Why*, that *Stay my Dear*,
> His disorder'd Locks he tare;
> And with rouling Eyes did glare,
> And his cruel Fate forswear.

After this, the lover's reply substitutes for his fury, as here described, a removed aesthetic appreciation of the situation, a Chinese detachment which in fact repudiates it:

> Gentler times for Love are ment:
> Who for parting pleasures strain
> Gather Roses in the rain,
> Wet themselves and spoil their Sent.

This prepares the way for the malicious turn of the last two verses, where 'Last night he with *Phlogis* slept; This night for *Dorinda* kept':

> Yet he does himself excuse;
> Nor indeed without a Cause.
> For, according to the Lawes,
> Why did *Chloe* once refuse?

In *Mourning*, the satire is the poet's, but it is achieved by the same means. The tears of the bereaved Chlora are first analysed in a series of purely intellectual conceits. The cynical bystanders suggest that she is weeping for joy rather than for grief and has already acquired a new lover. Then suddenly comes a magnificent invocation of tropical seas and pearls, a richness equally opposed to Chlora's mood of grief and to the too simple cynicism of her friends:

> How wide they dream! The *Indian* Slaves
> That sink for Pearl through Seas profound,
> Would find her Tears yet deeper Waves
> And of not one the bottom sound.

Sailors sound to test the firmness as well as the depth of the ground; pearls are most likely to be found on an oozy bed.

After this, it would be an anticlimax for the poet to pronounce flatly on the case: he withdraws into an equally profound reserve, which is more ironic, because more complex, than that of the lady's friends:

> I yet my silent Judgment keep,
> Disputing not what they believe:
> But sure as oft as Women weep,
> It is to be suppos'd they grieve.

Suppos'd either out of politeness or decency, or because nothing stronger than a supposition about human, and particularly feminine, sincerity is possible.

The delicate malice of this poem is strengthened if the *Chlora* whom it celebrates as weeping so copiously for her dead Strephon may be taken as the Chlora of *An Elegy Upon the Death of My Lord Francis Villiers*:[1]

> The matchlesse *Chlora* whose pure fires did warm
> His soule and only could his passions charme.[2]

She is also a prude and respects appearances:

> Yet she for honours tyrannous respect
> Her own desires did and his neglect.
> And like the Modest Plant at every touch
> Shrunk in her leaves and feard it was too much[3]

---

[1] This poem was found and first printed as Marvell's by H. M. Margoliouth. It has Marvell's tone and accent (e.g. cf. ll. 51–2, *Damon the Mower*, ll. 57–60; and ll. 119–20, *An Horatian Ode*, ll. 13–16). As Villiers was killed on 7 July 1648, the poem presumably belongs to that year. It is strongly Royalist, and includes hopeful expectations of the deaths of Cromwell and 'The long-deceived *Fairfax*' (ll. 13–16). The elegy for Lord Hastings which Marvell wrote a year later is a much better poem, and devoid of politics. It has been analysed by W. Empson, *Seven Types of Ambiguity* (Chatto and Windus, 1930), pp. 212–17.   [2] ll. 69–70.   [3] ll. 79–82.

It would be agreeable to think that the somewhat stiff and dull *Elegy* had such a sequel.

With Marvell's conversion to the Parliamentary party and his departure for the north, his poetry changed. *Upon Appleton House* contains some passages in his old emblematic, conceited style, particularly at the beginning and the end. It is clearly a transitional poem; its different parts are in different keys. It falls into six sections; the house (i–x), the history of Isabella Fairfax (xi–xxxv), the garden (xxxvi–xlvi), the meadow (xlvii–lx), the wood (lxi–lxxviii), evening by the river and Mary Fairfax (lxxix–xc). At the beginning and the end there is narrative and conceited description: in the middle are embedded passages in a new style, which seem to link on to other poems of this period, such as the series on the Mower.

Though the description of Nunappleton is worked out in mathematical terms which recall *Fleckno* (ll. 83–101) and though the passage at the end of the poem, about the Antipodes in shoes, has become notorious for its geometrical complexities (it is solid geometry too),[1] the most startling effects in the poem are probably those gained by using words in a new or transferred sense, a cross between a conceit and a pun:

> While the disjointed *Abbess* threads
> The gingling Chain-shot of her *Beads*....
>
> While at my Lines the Fishes twang....

[1] The idea of the 'Antipodes in Shoes' is taken from Cleveland's *Square Cap*, though, as applied to coracle fishermen, it is a just and and lively image. The geometric images here and in the description of the 'five imaginary Forts' are only a faint reflection of the geometry of *The Definition of Love*.

In these lines sensuous implication (muscular in the first case, oral in the second) is fresh and vivid. It is part of the new sensuous exuberance, which dominates the description of the meadow and the wood, but which in the early part of the poem appears disguised in the speeches recording the insidious temptations of the wicked Abbess, who tried to entice Isabella Thwaites from Sir William Fairfax.[1] Her epicureanism, though meant to be reprehensible, is too strong to be rejected completely. Like her abbey, it becomes the foundation of the later structure. This, for example, is a mock-heroic simile in which she describes the combination of 'Pleasure' and 'Duty' in living under a rule; it is intentionally burlesque:

> So through the mortal fruit we boyl
> The Sugars uncorrupting Oyl:
> And that which perisht while we pull,
> Is thus preserved clear and full.[2]

Yet the sense of rounded fruits and heavy syrup is as rich as that of *St Agnes' Eve* (it is largely a matter of alternating o's and u's, explosive p's and b's and smooth sibilants). The Abbess is presenting the very converse of *A Dialogue Between the Resolved Soul, and Created Pleasure*. She goes on to describe the bridebed where Isabella may 'lye as chast' with a sister nun:

> As Pearls together billeted.
> All Night embracing Arm in Arm,
> Like Chrystal pure with Cotton warm.[3]

[1] Isabella Thwaites brought Nunappleton into the family and therefore her story was peculiarly appropriate in a poem celebrating the house. She also brought into the family, not inappropriately, a beautiful illuminated MS. of the *Confessio Amantis*.

[2] XXII.   [3] XXIV.

The military verb has a surprising effect here, and sets off the softness of the cotton (like sugar, one of the rarities of the New World, and still a luxury for the discriminating). Neither effect is strictly proper in a Puritan poem.

The elegant gardens of General Fairfax are less exotic in suggestion, though he too has his rarities, such as the streaked tulip. But the gardens merge into the meadow, and here, though the wit remains, Nature is now felt as a whole; the great dominant metaphor—that of a battlefield—in which it is worked out shows that this is still an emblematic Nature, but Marvell's fresh and exact observation transforms it. The detail is curious and finely wrought, but the power of Nature felt as a whole is stronger than the detail, and for the first time Marvell's writing has become more than the sum of its parts.

The garden was laid out as a series of forts, and the military bees and flowers are commended for their good discipline:

> See how the Flow'rs, as at *Parade*,
> Under their *Colours* stand displaid:
> Each *Regiment* in order grows,
> That of the Tulip Pinke and Rose.[1]

This is not merely a compliment to the General; it stands for the civilized aspect of the landscape or of life. War in seventeenth-century England was a heroic and orderly defence of a good cause. Nevertheless, even in the hour of success, Marvell laments its neces-

[1] xxxix.

sity,[1] and the General's highest glory is that he gave up his command:

> For he did, with his utmost Skill,
> *Ambition* weed, but *Conscience* till.[2]

In this passage, where the garden reflects in itself Paradise, England, and Fairfax's own mind, there is the beginning of a new flexibility, a power to co-ordinate through metaphor and simile, which is the strength of Marvell's best poetry. It makes the power of such poems as *The Garden* and *Bermudas*. The metaphors no longer organize and limit the material as in *The unfortunate Lover*, nor provide momentary illumination, as in the roses of *Daphnis and Chloe* and the pearls of *Mourning*: they are generative, and from them comes the greater life of the poem. Marvell is not less alert, not less of a critic, because he has admitted here some of the gusto of the swain.

For out in the meadow, that 'Abbyss' of 'unfathomable Grass', things become more complicated. Men are lost in the grass: the grasshoppers squeak contemptuously 'from the Precipices tall Of the green spir's'. It is this change of scale which gives the sense of being submerged 'full fadom five':

> To see Men through this Meadow Dive,
> We wonder how they rise alive.
> As, under Water, none does know
> Whether he fall through it or go.[3]

The keynote here is *wonder*; the wit is now led by the subject, it is no longer playing upon it; the writing is

---

[1] See Chapter I, p. 4.   [2] XLV.   [3] XLVIII.

no longer so neatly explicit.[1] The tawny mowers come
'Walking on foot through a green Sea' and Death
(absent from the floral regiments) comes with them
as they 'Massacre the Grass' and one of them 'carves'
the corncrake:

> The Edge all bloody from its Breast
> He draws, and does his stroke detest;
> Fearing the Flesh untimely mow'd
> To him a Fate as black forebode.[2]

Then suddenly the battlefield is invoked, and with it
puns and gaiety, the critical-fantastic mood of the
garden. For the hay is all cut, and in the meadow they
only play at war:

> Where, as the Meads with Hay, the Plain
> Lyes quilted ore with Bodies slain:
> The Women that with forks it fling,
> Do represent the Pillaging.
>
> And now the careless Victors play,
> Dancing the Triumphs of the Hay.[3]

The meadow now begins to reflect the whole world:
it undergoes a whole series of transformations of a
curious and witty kind; it involves microscopes, the
plays of Davenant, a reminiscence of what the poet
had already written about the flooded meadows of
Holland.[4] He himself retreats into the wood, and it
is here that his own Metamorphosis comes:

---

[1] As, for instance, in Lovelace's poem on *The Grasshopper*, which has
its own charm.
[2] L.   [3] LIII, LIV.
[4] LIX, LX. Cf. *The Character of Holland*, ll. 23–36. This poem in its
present form probably dates from 1653, but it sounds as though it
had originally been written about the same time as *Fleckno*. It must
embody recollections of Marvell's first tour in Holland.

> Give me but Wings as they, and I
> Streight floting on the Air shall fly:
> Or turn me but, and you shall see
> I was but an inverted Tree.[1]

It is not altogether serious, but there are other signs
of Ovidian encroachment: the plants thrust themselves on him like lovers: oak leaves embroider, and
ivy 'licks, and clasps, and curles, and hales'. The ex-
citement of the poem grows, because Marvell feels
that 'in this yet green, yet growing Ark' he has a
microcosm, a whole world. This is explicitly stated
only at the very end of the poem:

> Your lesser *World* contains the same.
> But in more decent Order tame;
> *You Heaven's Center, Nature's Lap.*
> *And Paradice's only Map.*[2]

It explains, if it cannot justify, the conceits about
the Antipodes in shoes, the exhilarated sense that an
illustration for everything, a mirror-reflection of everything, can be found in Nunappleton.

Upon Appleton House is uneven, muddled, but it is
positive. The personal security which is the root of the
feeling is given in the military metaphors which have
been used all along to stand for reason and order; and
it is against that fashionable world which was the
subject of the earlier verse that the warfare is directed.
In the following passage, for example, the masculine
force of the last couplet implies complete security:

> How safe, methinks, and strong, behind
> These Trees have I incamp'd my Mind;

[1] LXXI.   [2] LXXXXVI.

> Where Beauty, aiming at the Heart,
> Bends in some Tree its useless Dart;
> And where the World no certain Shot
> Can make, or me it toucheth not.
> But I on it securely play,
> And gaul its Horsemen all the Day.[1]

The magnificent evening piece which closes the poem leaves the poet still strongly encamped. This does not prevent his paying courtly compliments to the General and to his pupil, Mary Fairfax. For the critic and the swain have joined forces.

This union can be seen more clearly in the series of Mowers' Songs, which seem to have developed from the mowing scene in *Upon Appleton House*. The Mower is a special variant of the stock Swain, more English and also more of a person. Sometimes he is a simple countryman (*Damon the Mower*, v–vii), and sometimes his simplicity is the last reward of sophistication (*The Mower against Gardens*).

This poem begins gravely enough: Man has sinned, and brought Death into the world. He has infected all Nature with his own 'luxurious' vice: every flower has learnt deceitful allurements:

> With strange perfumes he did the Roses taint.
> And Flow'rs themselves were taught to paint.

—the same sins against which the poet had to encamp his mind. But the detail with which these horticultural crimes are described suggests anything but indifference: the interest is that of a gardener. The wit of the writing is directly opposed to the Puritan asceticism it

[1] LXXVI.

D

claims to advocate: it is airy and fanciful: such a line as

> His green *Seraglio* has its Eunuchs too

amuses by a sophisticated playfulness.[1]

Then suddenly the standards of Nature are more seriously invoked; they are equally far from asceticism, but instead of the elaborate fancies of the garden they have a fresh sensuousness:

> 'Tis all enforc'd; the Fountain and the Grot;
>   While the sweet Fields do lye forgot:
> Where willing Nature does to all dispence
>   A wild and fragrant Innocence.

'Willing Nature' may be free with her favours, but she remains 'plain and pure'. The garden gods are alive in the meadows, while the gardener has only their statues; those amorous creatures, the '*Fauns* and *Faryes*', till the fields, but this because they are lucky rather than because they take any such pains as the gardener does.

The elegance and wit of the poem depend at first on pretending to denounce what is really enjoyed in a 'witty' manner; but the conclusion gains its power

[1] Two lines have puzzled all the editors: 'And in the Cherry he does Nature vex, To procreate without a Sex.' This cannot refer to grafting, which has been mentioned already. It may possibly refer to the *stoneless* Cherry. See William Lawson, *A New Orchard and Garden...* (1618). The real sexual organs of plants were not known till 1676, and by a pun it would be easy to take the stone as the 'sex' of the cherry. *Procreate* means *produce* (*O.E.D.* s.v. 4) and its subject is Man, or rather 'he'. 'Man vexes Nature by producing a cherry which is not merely a Eunuch, but sexless from the beginning.' Lawson, whose book is the first to consider gardening in the north of England in particular, mentions both the stoneless cherry and the stoneless plum.

from the resolution of the discord. It is as delicate as the beginning and more satisfying. Neither attitude is rustic: and the Mower's occupation is only relevant in so far as he makes a clean sweep both of the narrow ascetic and the mere fine gentleman.

The other Mower's Songs are love poems, but not in a serious sense. The lady is cruel; but she is not very important. It is Nature who supplies the positive feelings, and with whom the Mower unites himself:

> My Mind was once the true survey
> Of all these Medows fresh and gay;
> And in the greenness of the Grass
> Did see its Hopes as in a Glass...
>
> And thus, ye Meadows, which have been
> Companions of my thoughts more green,
> Shall now the Heraldry become
> With which I shall adorn my Tomb.[1]

The attitude of this poem is much more complicated than that of any of the others: but this is compensated by the poem's being the only one with a burden, which, as Margoliouth says, reproduces the long sweep of the scythe, and relates the poem directly to the Mower's occupation, smoothing away the teasing arguments:

> For *Juliana* comes, and She
> What I do to the Grass, does to my Thoughts and Me.

'My Thoughts and Me' is not however the language of a simple swain; this rustic is not so simple as tradition would suggest, but neither is he quite in control, in full possession of the attitude implied by the whole

[1] *The Mower's Song*. Cf. p. 59, n.

poem. In *The Mower to the Glo-Worms*, the tone is lowered, rusticity emphasized:

> Ye Country Comets, that portend
> No War, nor Princes funeral,
> Shining unto no higher end
> Then to presage the Grasses fall;

but again the conceits are dexterous and not at all rustic. It is the scene itself which supplies most of the positive feeling in these poems, as here where we are obscurely reminded that all Flesh is grass, and as at the end of *Damon the Mower*, where we see 'By his own Sythe, the Mower mown'—the Clown as Death:[1]

> Only for him no Cure is found,
> Whom *Julianas* Eyes do wound.
> 'Tis death alone that this must do:
> For Death thou art a Mower too.

The accident happens but by careless chance: it tempers the richness of the July scene, but the lover's conceit, very properly, makes Death no greater thing than a remedy against Juliana.

The dates of Marvell's two greatest love poems are uncertain; *To his Coy Mistress* suggests a Yorkshire rather than a London setting (l. 7) and the geometry of *The Definition of Love* improves on that of *Upon Appleton House*. They are far in advance of the earlier group, but they do not seem to fit very well with the religious and political poems of 1653–8: there is a certain taut intellectualism about them which is not

[1] See W. Empson, *Some Versions of Pastoral* (Chatto and Windus, 1935), p. 129. Death comes into all the Mower's Songs: *Damon the Mower*, ll. 87–8; *The Mower against Gardens*, ll. 5–8; *The Mower to the Glo-Worms*, ll. 5–6; *The Mower's Song*, ll. 25–8.

so obvious later. The style has even more strength than ease.

In theme and method they are completely contrasted: the one magnificently concrete, the other as completely transcendental; the one astonishing in its variety, the other in its consistency.

To his Coy Mistress opens with the play of conceits, the whole macrocosm is seen in Metamorphosis: time's changes are jested with:

> My vegetable Love should grow[1]
> Vaster then Empires, and more slow.

The 'long Loves Day' then turns into Eternity: Metamorphosis is accepted in its keenest implications:

> ...then Worms shall try
> That long preserv'd Virginity:
> And your quaint Honour turn to dust.

When this is accepted, the very knowledge and the assurance that come from its acceptance turn the present moment into an eternity, focusing into it all the power of the many thousand years it ought to be:

> Now therefore, while the youthful hew
> Sits on thy skin like morning lew,[2]...
> Let us roll all our Strength, and all
> Our sweetness, up into one Ball.

---

[1] The common misunderstanding of 'vegetable Love' is a typical example of how Marvell is misread. 'Vegetable' had much stronger metaphysical than culinary associations in the seventeenth century, as in the phrase 'vegetable soul' or Milton's 'vegetable gold' even. The nearest modern equivalent is perhaps 'sentient'. For an interesting early reminiscence of this verse, see *The Spectator*, No. 89.

[2] *Lew* is the heat haze, the 'bloom' which the dew makes on the landscape early in a warm day, and this transient, warm bloom is

The Sphere is the commonest symbol of Eternity: this is no simple doctrine of *carpe diem*. The 'am'rous birds of prey' do not merely make the best of Time; they conquer it. But it is Marvell's most direct and immediate apprehensions of the here-and-now which include past and future. The final paradox suggests that though the lovers cannot control Time, yet *a fortiori* it is their energy alone that supplies the motive power of existence whereby Time is created. (Compare Donne's *The Sunne Rising*.)

> Thus, though we cannot make our Sun
> Stand still, yet we will make him run.

They are not Joshuas, they are gods.

This is not a flamboyant boast; it is a metaphysical statement parallel to that of *The Definition of Love*,—

> ...Loves whole World on us doth wheel.

But while in *To his Coy Mistress* the power is finally concentrated into a moment, the instant of creative strife in which Time is devoured, in *The Definition of Love* there is no temporal process and indeed no external reference. Even the Lady seems only a postulated figure, a force of Love, a point on the graph. It is the situation rather than the feelings that count, for they are past the stage of having 'feelings'. The story is given in terms of direct sensation; it is defined by imagery and rhythm alone, without any circumstantial account.

---

compared with the *duveté* of his mistress's complexion: something very delicate, shown only in a particular light or a particular posture.

The title itself presents one paradox: Love, the unruliest of the passions, is to receive a *definition*. This was a new noun, the earliest known use of it being that of Milton in 1645: it would sound much more technical to a contemporary of Marvell than it does to us. Marvell was using the new interests in geometry, which went with rationalism, and the opposition to Plato, in a poem on Platonic love: this is the second paradox. The theme of the poem supplies the third.

This theme is that material Fate and spiritual Love, though apparently in complete opposition, are in reality two aspects of the same situation:

> Magnanimous Despair alone
> Could show me so divine a thing.

If 'the Stars' were not so completely opposed, the love could not reach such heroic stature.

Nevertheless, this transcendental love is presented through direct sensuous channels, through imagery and rhythm. The sense of tension, of muscular effort, appears in the image of Hope beating its tinsel wing between Heaven and Hell, whilst the 'extended Soul', like the Ether, reaches up to its 'high' object. (*Extended Soul* is another paradox, extension being the attribute of matter.) The iron wedges of Fate are perhaps meant to be magnetic. Fate will not let the lovers 'close'; there is almost a feeling of crucifixion:

> And yet I quickly might arrive
> Where my extended Soul is fixt,
> But Fate does Iron wedges drive,[1]
> And alwaies crouds it self betwixt.

---

[1] This recalls Horace, *Car.* I, xxxv, 17–20: 'te semper anteit

The heavily emphasized antitheses support the imagery here: the two halves of the verse balance like the 'Two perfect Loves'.[1]

The lovers next become the 'distant Poles' on which the whole world of Love revolves; without a convulsion which will 'Strike flat the thicke Rotundity o' th' world' they cannot meet. The next geometric simile also carries on the feeling of tension:

> As Lines so Loves *oblique* may well
> Themselves in every Angle greet:
> But ours so truly *Paralel*,
> Though infinite can never meet.

Perhaps there is a reference to an idea Marvell states elsewhere,[2] that a straight line produced to infinity becomes a circle. In that sense the lovers may say that they

> roll all our Strength, and all
> Our sweetness, up into one Ball.

In the words of the next verse, it is

> the Conjunction of the Mind,
> And Opposition of the Stars.

The direct unmetaphorical reference to the *Stars* and the continuance of the metaphor in the puns on *Conjunctions* and *Oppositions* releases the tension: the problem is solved because fully stated.

Yet the metaphors from geometry are precise and

saeva Necessitas/clavos trabalis et cuneos manu/gestans aena, nec severus/uncus abest liquidumque plumbum.'

[1] The antitheses give weight and hard energy to the rhythm: the many suspended clauses and inversions give tension; e.g. 'nor lets them close'; 'And, us to joyn'. Cf. Donne, *Valediction Forbidding Mourning*, ll. 20–36.

[2] Grosart, vol. III, pp. 146, 314.

intellectual, in distinction to the strong but unfocused feeling of muscular tension, for muscular imagery is the most powerful and immediate kind, being bound up with the simplest and most instinctive habits. The poem is a triumph of organization as well as of strength; and in this, as well as in the theme—that material Fate and spiritual Love, though they do not interact, reflect each other,—recalls momentarily the methods and theories of Marvell's great contemporary, Spinoza.

These two love poems are the most strictly concentrated poetry which Marvell ever wrote. But the concentration implies intensity, and his most characteristic work is concentrated without being intense; the material is smoothly blended, the transitions from one level to another are managed with the spontaneity of a perfectly disciplined art, so that there is a deceptive air of ease about such poems as *The Garden*, *A Dialogue between the Soul and Body* and *Bermudas*.

This chapter may be concluded with a survey of some poems which have affinities with the Nunappleton verse but which point forward to the fuller style of Marvell's maturity.

The Nymph complaining for the death of her Faun opens with straightforward and charming naturalism; it ends by drawing largely on *The Song of Solomon* and its identification of the fawn with Christ. The nymph is at once amusing and touching and aesthetically delightful (rather like Henry James' young girls).[1] She is firm in her pious conviction that the wanton troopers who have shot her fawn will be punished:

[1] Cf. *Upon Appleton House*, L–LIII.

> Ev'n Beasts must be with justice slain;
> Else Men are made their *Deodands*.[1]

(A deodand is itself a beast or quite inanimate: thus men may be degraded below the beasts: the force of the technical ecclesiastical term as used by the little nymph can only be appreciated later.)

In the opening part of the poem the fawn is a substitute for Sylvio, the unconstant lover whose present it was:

> Said He, look how your Huntsman here
> Hath taught a Faun to hunt his *Dear*.
> But *Sylvio* soon had me beguil'd.
> This waxed tame; while he grew wild,
> And quite regardless of my Smart,
> Left me his Faun, but took his Heart.[2]

It is not certain whether the nymph is meant to see the puns or not; they certainly give the effect of rallying her upon this grief. But her simplicity becomes a religious purity when she comes directly to the subject of the fawn:

> Among the beds of Lillyes, I
> Have sought it oft, where it should lye;...
> For, in the flaxen Lillies shade,
> It like a bank of Lillies laid.
> Upon the Roses it would feed,
> Until its Lips ev'n seem'd to bleed:...
> Had it liv'd long, it would have been
> Lillies without, Roses within.[3]

My beloved is mine, and I am his: he feedeth among the lillies.

Untill the day breake, and the shadowes flee away: turne my beloved and be thou like a Roe, or a yong Hart, upon the mountaines of Bether....

[1] ll.16–17.　　[2] ll. 31–6.　　[3] ll. 77 ff.

Thy two breasts, are like two yong Roes, that are twinnes, which feed among the lillies.

Untill the day breake, and the shadowes flee away, I will get mee to the mountaines of myrrhe, and to the hill of frankincense....

My beloved is gone downe into his garden, to the beds of spices, to feede in the gardens, and to gather lillies.

I am my beloveds, & my beloved is mine: he feedeth among the lillies....

I am the rose of Sharon, and the lillie of the valleys.[1]

The whiteness of the fawn is insisted on throughout the poem: as well as being stressed in *The Song of Solomon* it is of course symbolic of the Agnus Dei. It is this identification which allows the transition to martyrdom:

> O help! O help! I see it faint:
> And dye as calmely as a Saint.
> See how it weeps. The Tears do come
> Sad, slowly dropping like a Gumme.
> So weeps the wounded Balsome: so
> The holy Frankincense doth flow.[2]

It would be difficult to do this now without being blasphemous: it is a very complete example of a hierarchy of love, but to relate is not to obliterate differences: Marvell's very nicety of control of the transitions has impressed on the reader the need for

[1] *The Song of Solomon*, II, 16–17; IV, 5–6; VI, 2–3; II, 1.

[2] Ll. 93–8. Cf. the earlier lines, referring to the troopers, who now seem to have slain that which would have redeemed them: 'There is not such another in The World, to offer for their Sin' (ll. 23–4). The whole poem may be related to the death and metamorphosis of Fida's hind in William Browne's *Britannia's Pastorals* (Bk. I, Songs 4 and 5). Browne's nymph represents religious Faith and the hind, Truth. The new connections with such poets as Browne and Giles Fletcher are important and will be discussed in the next chapter.

making fine distinctions. It is equally implied that the two ends of the scale *are* related. The love of the girl for her fawn is taken to be a reflection of the love of the Church for Christ.

Such comparisons could be made by simpler poets than Marvell. In Giles Fletcher's *Christ's Triumph after Death*, the Ascension is compared with the snatching away of Ganymede by Jove's eagle. This is to begin from the other end of the hierarchy; but Fletcher saw no impropriety in relating archetype and ectype, though to many modern minds he must seem either very short-sighted or rather obscene.

The range of feeling in this short poem is something new in Marvell. The rather bitter wit of his early verse has led through the tense and excited verse of *Upon Appleton House* to this gentle and sobered blend of amusement, affection and religion. The heroine too has changed from a court lady to a Puritan country girl.

This range can be seen in his other poems about children; for instance, *Young Love*, where the balance is beautifully maintained between the courtly gravity of the address and the suggestion of some romping game like *Ring a ring o' Roses*:

> So, to make all Rivals vain,
>   Now I crown thee with my Love:
> Crown me with thy Love again,
>   And we both shall Monarchs prove.

In *The Picture of little T. C....*[1] the balance is more

[1] If H. M. Margoliouth's conjecture (*Modern Language Review*, vol. xvii, 1922) is correct, and little T. C. is Theophila Cornewall, baptized in

complex. The poem is not all addressed to little T. C.,
and its tone has therefore more variety. It is delightful
to see the old mood of ironic gallantry turned to producing a mock heroic picture of little T. C.'s future
conquests:

> O then let me in time compound,
> And parly with those conquering Eyes;
> Ere they have try'd their force to wound,
> Ere, with their glancing wheels, they drive
> In Triumph over Hearts that strive,
> And them that yield but more despise.

But the turn of the verse:

> Let me be laid,
> Where I may see thy Glories from some Shade

suggests death; and the deadly glancing wheels become rather more serious than they have been. Finally,
when all Nature is joining in the homage to little T. C.,
that same Nature is suddenly presented as threatening
and cruel: little T. C.'s power, celebrated in four verses,
is suddenly confronted with the danger springing out of
that power itself:

> But O young beauty of the Woods,
> Whom Nature courts with fruit and flow'rs,
> Gather the Flow'rs, but spare the Buds;
> Lest *Flora* angry at thy crime,
> To kill her Infants in their prime,
> Do quickly make th'Example Yours;
> And, ere we see,
> Nip in the blossome all our hopes and Thee.

This puts the courtesies of the first verse in the right

September 1644, the poem could be reasonably dated when Theophila
was about eight or ten years old, i.e. 1652–4.

perspective; makes them playful but not mock courtesies; gives, in the most reckless of the poem's conceits, the measure of direct feeling behind it. It is indeed the final courtesy of the poem; the uncalculated tribute to little T. C., not as she will be, but as she is.[1]

[1] Gerard Manley Hopkins has based a poem on a similar theme; it too was inspired by a picture—*On the Portrait of Two Beautiful Young People*. The peripeteia of the last verse of *The Picture of little T. C.* was first noted in E. M. W. Tillyard's *Poetry Direct and Oblique* (Chatto and Windus, 1934), pp. 204–5.

III

CONTEMPLATION AND ACTION

Not many poems can be dated with confidence as having been written between 1653 and 1658. The panegyric on Blake's naval triumphs belongs to 1653; the poem on the first anniversary of Cromwell's government to the end of 1655; the songs for the marriage of Mary Cromwell to November 1657. There are also the group of Latin poems to Oliver St John, Dr Ingelo, and the verses for the Queen of Sweden.

The only poem not specifically political which seems to belong to this time is *Bermudas*, which was probably inspired by recollections of Oxenbridge's journey to the West Indies. The connections in theme and mood between *Bermudas* and *The Garden* are close enough to suggest that they were not widely separated in time. There is some evidence of a kind which allows inferences to be made about Marvell's interests during these years: and it would seem reasonable to place here such poems as are separated in tone and temper from those known or assumed to belong to 1651–3.

At Eton he returned to the world of affairs, and also to an atmosphere much more positively Puritan than that of Nunappleton. The effect of his connection with John Hales can be estimated only from his use of the Tract on Schism in *The Rehearsal Transpros'd*, when, at nearly twenty years' distance, it was still considerable. Oxenbridge was an enthusiast, but he was a learned man. At Eton, Marvell would return to a more academic milieu, and it was to be expected that the speculative tone of such poems as *A Dialogue between the Soul and Body* should represent the deepening of his own interests.

In addition to the change of interest, there is also a change in his style and his models. As in his prose he was to pass from the brilliant but disjointed wit of *The Rehearsal Transpros'd* to the tempered and consistent style of *The Growth of Popery*, so in his poetry he seems to have progressed from Clevelandism to something very like Spenserianism. How far Milton was responsible for introducing him to the tradition of William Browne and the Fletchers it is difficult to say; but his own use of Spenserian conceptions in *The Picture of little T. C.* and *The Garden* gives to his poetry a depth and resonance it had hitherto lacked.

This does not mean that as a poet he learned more from the Spenserians than from Donne; but it was the Spenserians who were the chief custodians of the old symbolic view of Nature as the Divine Hieroglyph. Its English origins were medieval, it was active in Shakespeare, the Elizabethan dramatists,[1] and Sir Thomas Browne, whose meditations on the Quincunx were written in 1658. This *Weltanschauung*, already indicated at the end of *Upon Appleton House*, had grown naturally out of what we have called Marvell's em-

[1] See the article by Basil Willey in *Studies presented to Sir Herbert Grierson* (Oxford, 1938). The 'Spenserians' were mostly 'Sons of Ben'.

blematic technique, and it came to dominate his poetry. During the later seventeenth century natural science removed the supports from this older conception of Nature; and Marvell ceased to write poetry. Perhaps the political shock of the Restoration might not have been overwhelming, but for these larger changes of thought.

Politics are for Marvell part of the natural order of the world: from the rational and most conscious organizations of corporate man to the return of the seasons and the precession of the heavens there is a continuum. The correlation of man's life with the natural order of day and night, the order of the spheres, the rhythm of the year, means that the terms are poetically interchangeable, and the strength and solidity of Marvell's work lies in the relation between one level and the other, which distinguishes them while bringing them together.

The Nature which Marvell knew was plainly different from that which Wordsworth, for example, knew. The stars still rained influences, the earth still gave out humours: there was no such thing as inanimate nature and no possibility of a pathetic fallacy.[1] The following passage, taken from Ralph Austen's *Dialogue...between the Husbandman and the Fruit Trees* (1676), will show that some of Marvell's airiest conceits are based on a conception literally interpreted by the devout:

Men must *discourse with Fruit Trees*, having learned to

[1] The phrase could only be improperly applied to the attitudes of *Twicknam Garden* and *Lycidas*, for example.

E

understand *their Language*, which, though it be not Articulate, and distinct to the *outward sense of hearing*, in the sound of words, yet they speake plainly and distinctly to the *inward sense*, the *understanding*: The soul hath its *sences* as well as the body: the soul doth really *hear*, see, etc. as well as the body: so that we may learn from Fruit Trees, many good lessons, and usefull instructions: they being Creatures, that are alwaies speaking, and alwaies speak the truth, both for the glory of God and the good of man.[1]

This seems to fit in with Marvell's studies among the woods at Nunappleton, where his linguistic works were extended to the tongues of birds and trees:

> Already I begin to call
> In their most learned Original...
> Thrice happy he who, not mistook,
> Hath read in *Natures mystick Book*.

Marvell did not always treat these interconnections so lightly: for instance, in *A Dialogue between the Soul and Body* he uses seriously the exact parallelism between the senses of the body and the senses of the soul, together with their common relation to 'green trees that in the forest grew'. In the seventeenth century Nature could be interpreted in a detailed way and in almost a matter of fact frame of mind. It was not only the theologians, but also the scientists, who were ready to see the whole of inanimate nature as a channel of mystical experience.[2]

[1] *Epistle to the Reader*, pp. 4–5. Cf. *Clorinda and Damon*.

[2] See John Read, *Prelude to Chemistry* (Bell, 1936). The whole of inanimate nature was seen by the Hermeticists in the manner illustrated by the following quotation (from an experiment for heating gold with antimony): 'Then hand over the King to the ravening Wolf, and that three times, and stoutly burn the Wolf in fire' (p. 201).

The sun and moon were still 'the male and female principle' to scientists: and chemistry, both in conceptions and in terminology, was strictly emblematic. During Marvell's lifetime the work of such men as Boyle and John Ray killed a great deal of old belief; but Marvell grew up in the old order.

To illustrate from a subject in which Marvell was specially interested—the Puritanical Ralph Austen, having published in 1653 a horticultural treatise on *The Uses of an Orchard*, found no incongruity in following it with a second part on *The Spiritual Uses of an Orchard*, in which by a liberal use of scripture he advanced the theological claims of plums and pears, and drew excellent moral examples from grafting and cross-breeding. Austen was a professional gardener; but as he trespassed on the theologians' ground, so they retaliated. The Catholics, and in particular the Jesuits, used emblematic methods of instruction; the English Jesuit Henry Hawkins, for instance, in his *Partheneia Sacra* saw reflected in a garden all the virtues of the Virgin Mary, and worked out an elaborate system of symbolism mainly in terms of flowers.[1] This, for example, is from the *Character* of the Heliotropion:

It is even the Eye, & nothing els but the Eye, to behold the Sun; which she never shuts, til he sincks down in *Tethis*' bed; where, being drowned over head and eares, she wincks and shrowds herself the while, in

---

[1] We are indebted to Miss Rosemary Freeman for this reference. She has also referred us to E. M.'s *Ashrea*.... (1665), which illustrates the Beatitudes by emblems of trees.

the thin eyelids of her leaves, to meditate upon him. It is the Arsenal of crimson-flags displayed to the *Pithian Apollo*, in despite of *Mars*, whom she adores as God of Armes as wel as Bookes; wheras *Mars*, if you take him from his speare and shield, can neither write nor reade. It is the *Gnomon* of the Garden, a Dial artificially made in hearbs, to expresse al the howers of the day; a verie needle, pointing to its radiant Starre; which being so restles as it is, makes her as restles everie whit; with this difference only, that he measures infinit degrees of Heavens, and she as manie points.... She is so amourous, & dotes so much upon him, that she can not live without his conversation; which she hath so much, as she almost is turn'd and quite metamorphosied into him, and now become already in the Garden, what he is in his Zodiack, the true and real flower of the Sun, or Sun of Flowers, as he himself the Sun of starres, or that great Starre they call a Sun.... It is even the *Daphne* of flowers, whom *Phœbus* followes al the day; and, if she fly, she hath her eye on her shoulder, to looke behind her, as she runnes.[1]

This passage shows the same blend of religious sentiment, natural observation, classical mythology and symbolic method as some of the poems of Marvell, particularly *The Garden* and *On a Drop of Dew*. Where Marvell improves on the Jesuit and on most of the Spenserians is in his power to enliven by contrast his different material, as we have already seen in *The Nymph complaining for the death of her Faun*. If his *Bermudas* be compared with Drayton's *To the Virginian Voyage* it will be clear that the difference is not in stature but development. The two poets also invite comparison in their pastoral songs.

[1] *Partheneia Sacra* (1633), pp. 48–9.

The most complex, though not the most complicated, of his poems is *The Garden*, which comes
nearest of all his works to being metaphysical in the
strict sense: it might have as epigraph 'The solution
of the problem of life is seen in the vanishing of this
problem'. Ambition, Love, Religion are included in
the poem, not as subjects to be surveyed (and therein
lies the difference from the poems of Nunappleton),
but as part of his own living experience, as it is here
contemplated.

The first two verses are a contemplation of Ambition; the man of 'uncessant Labours' becomes
narrowed and warped, whereas Nature could have
developed him more completely:

> ...all Flow'rs and all Trees do close
> To weave the Garlands of repose.

The Earthly Paradise is regained, though the
Quiet and Innocence found there are a complex
satisfaction of the whole man, not the spontaneous
and simple feelings dependent either on inexperience
or privation.

The next two verses treat of Desire, first the polite
and conventional feelings of the 'Fond Lovers, cruel
as their Flame' who cut names on the trees; then the
feelings of the poet, who, though he disposes of the
mistress, retains in himself all the warm and supple
moods of the lover:

> No white nor red was ever seen
> So am'rous as this lovely green.[1]

[1] Cf. *Love's Labour's Lost*, 1. 2. 81. *Green* was the colour of lovers, and *red and white* a common, almost proverbial phrase for beauty in a woman, e.g. *The Rape of Lucrece*, sts. 1–x.

The adjectives of the second line are enough to
show that, even if the heraldic interpretation of
colours should have been overlooked, the state of being
a lover is not foregone. The full adaptation of the
lover's customs to the garden has a delicate and ardent
force:

> Fair Trees! where s'eer your barkes I wound,
> No Name shall but your own be found....
> The *Gods*, that mortal Beauty chase,
> Still in a Tree did end their race.

Race is a pun on *contest* and *family, seed*. He finds, as
the gods found, that the only lasting satisfaction for
the instincts is an activity which does not employ them
for their original purpose. Apollo hunted Daphne
for the laurel crown of Poetry and Pan sped after
Syrinx to capture Music.[1]

The flowers and trees do not behave in the least like
Daphne and Syrinx; it is they who woo the poet:

> What wond'rous Life is this I lead!
> Ripe Apples drop about my head;
> The Luscious Clusters of the Vine
> Upon my Mouth do crush their Wine;
> The Nectaren, and curious Peach,
> Into my hands themselves do reach;
> Stumbling on Melons, as I pass,
> Insnar'd with Flow'rs, I fall on Grass.

[1] A translation of Marvell's Latin version of this poem brings this
out more unambiguously: 'Who is not enthralled by the graces of a
maiden's beauty? though she be whiter than snow and redder than
scarlet dye, yet in my judgment your fresh green virtue would surpass
her.... Here Love puts off his wings and walks sandalled, laying aside
his slackened bow and hissing arrows, and lowers his torch, nor ever
seeks to tyrannize.... The Gods above rejoice when the tyrant loses
his heat, and maybe they, versed in all nymphs and goddesses, are

After the very full and conscious dealing with the gods, it is clear that the greater satisfaction here includes the less, and Marvell emphasizes the point. The weight of the whole Spenserian tradition, in which Metamorphosis is the poetical answer to the decay of beauty and the triumph of time, is behind the exultation of this transformation. In the garden life is perpetually renewed, as it was for Spenser in the Gardens of Adonis.[1]

In the next verse, the Metamorphosis is carried a step further, and Nature herself suffers a sea-change in the Mind:

> Mean while, the Mind, from pleasure less,
> Withdraws into its happiness:
> The Mind, that Ocean where each kind
> Does streight its own resemblance find;
> Yet it creates, transcending these,
> Far other Worlds, and other Seas;
> Annihilating all that's made
> To a green Thought in a green Shade.[2]

now better satisfied each with his tree. Jupiter deserts his wife, and possesses the long lived oak: Juno was never so jealous of any other. No traces pollute the Lemnian bed: Mars does not remember Venus if the ash be by. Phoebus pressed hard on the track of lovely Daphne that she might become a laurel. And if goat footed Pan chased the fleeing Syrinx it was that he might find a singing reed.'

[1] Cf. also such stories as those of Marina and Walla in *Britannia's Pastorals*. For the tradition in general see D. Bush, *Mythology and the Renaissance Tradition* (Minnesota and Oxford, 1932).

[2] *Transcending* means both to overshoot and to exceed, but not to be independent. This high state of contemplation seems to spring from the idea that *for the mind of the spectator* some material things can actually take the substance of other material things: see *The Definition of Love* and *Eyes and Tears*, and the burlesques, *The Character of Holland*, ll. 23–36, *Upon Appleton House*, LX: here there are nymphs turned to trees, and an earthly garden to Paradise (that idea is also in the last verse of *Upon Appleton House*). In Nature itself things cannot take each other's

There must be a green shade, otherwise no green thought: that is, he only achieves the power of complete detachment through the instrumentality of that particular time and place.

It is again by means of the concrete features of the Garden—the baptismal fountain,[1] the tree of knowledge—that he achieves the final Metamorphosis, the escape from his limited personal self:

> Here at the Fountains sliding foot,
> Or at some Fruit-trees mossy root,
> Casting the Bodies Vest aside,
> My Soul into the boughs does glide.

The spiritual use of fruit trees has been clearly demonstrated here. The process is complete. At first there were the 'uncessant Labours' of the active life, and a long search for quiet and innocence; then in Daphne and Syrinx mortal beauty transmuted into permanence, as in the figures on Keats' Grecian Urn. Then a green thought concentrated all existence to an infinitesimal point of time. Now the soul escapes altogether from the flesh: it flies into the boughs, where, 'like a Bird it sits, and sings'.

As Daphne was the culmination of the classical, this is the culmination of the Christian imagery of the poem. The phenomenal, the temporal, become undulations in the luminous wings: the soul remains on earth though preening for heaven:

> And, till prepar'd for longer flight,
> Waves in its Plumes the various Light.

places—*penetration of substance* is impossible (*Fleckno*, ll. 97–101; *An Horatian Ode*, ll. 40–44)—so that this theory is idealistic.

[1] Cf. *Clorinda and Damon*, ll. 13–16.

The next verse returns to the 'happy Garden-state' of Innocence, but in a lighter, gayer mood.[1] Man and Nature have redeemed each other and have achieved a kind of union. Eden itself is Lilith and Eve an intruder.

The last verse marks partly the metamorphosis of Time, and partly the return to the world suggested by the gaiety of the verse before. It is far more definitely concerned with the garden as a local and temporal fact. The poet is looking at a floral sundial, a most sophisticated and artificial toy; and one which nowadays serves to remind the reader that the formalities of a seventeenth-century garden would not be at all likely to induce an ecstasy in him. It was a matter of 'knots' and parterres, and alleys; and only the emblematic mind could be led into a state of contemplation among its geometric fancies.[2]

The poet has returned to earth and to the external facts of the garden, with his compliment to the gardener, and is 'computing his time'. He can now afford, perhaps, to include even the trivialities he had to begin by excluding: he comes back to earth

---

[1] The implications of *State* include *temper, condition of mind or feeling*, and the ecclesiastical and political senses. The ecclesiastical sense perhaps dominates here.

[2] It is perhaps worth noting that floral dials were particularly popular in the West Indies, where they were marked out in myrtle and cypress macrocarpa, according to William Hughes in his *Flower Garden* (1692). Oxenbridge may have brought this special fashion back with him: though indeed Marvell might have seen floral dials at Cambridge, for there was one in the Master's garden at Pembroke, and another in the Fellows' garden at Queens' (see Loggan, *Cantabrigia Illustrata* (1690)).

refreshed—there is humility but also exhilaration, in
his recognition of his place in the scheme of things:

> How well the skilful Gardner drew
> Of flow'rs and herbes this Dial new;

—not only did he make the dial well, but it was well
that he did do so. And it is *new*; not merely a novelty
but with some of the 'wond'rous' quality of that
'happy Garden-state' of Innocence. In it the milder
sun runs through a *fragrant* zodiac (Marvell's Latin
has a kind of pun in *fragrantia signa*; they would
normally be *flagrantia*, burning). Time is now dependent on living things, instead of living things
being subject to time: the 'industrious Bee' correlates
with the 'uncessant Labours' of the first verse. Time
is not here something to be reckoned, but to be experienced; it is told by the living flowers and the bee
'computes' it no less well than men.

The fullness and power of this poem is of a different
order from that of *Upon Appleton House*. The language
has no longer the same epigrammatic brilliance but it
has much greater implication and weight. Almost every
word in the poem has an idiomatic life of its own, and
Marvell is here 'throwing the strongest stress on the
naked thew and sinew of the English Language'. The
vocabulary has the full concreteness of the early seventeenth century, and something of the later seventeenth
century's syntactical smoothness.

In *Bermudas* the richness of the language and of the
landscape is part of the religious jubilation of the
poem, 'An holy and a chearful Note'. The dominant

influences are obviously the 104th Psalm[1] and the *Benedicite*; but the isle, as well as being a kind of earthly paradise, is a glorified England too, and the whole vision is given a framework by being put into a song, and set in a harmonic combination of singing and rowing:

> And all the way, to guide their Chime,
> With falling Oars they kept the time.

They might be expected to sing in order to keep their stroke in rowing; but on the contrary the useful is subordinated, though it is there, just as the beauties of the isle turn out to be nearly all of a practical kind too. The richness of this Earthly Paradise is of the same kind as that of *The Garden*, and the plants thrust themselves on man in the same way, but here through Divine benevolence, not in natural exuberance:

> He makes the Figs our mouths to meet;
> And throws the Melons at our feet.
> But Apples plants of such a price,
> No Tree could ever bear them twice.
> With Cedars, chosen by his hand,
> From *Lebanon*, he stores the Land.

This suggests 'that dear and happy Isle', the triumphant England of 1653 rather than the remote Bermudas.[2] But in his religious poetry Marvell always

[1] Cf. especially verses 10–28.
[2] Cf. *The Rehearsal Transpros'd*, Part II, pp. 174–5 (Grosart, vol. III, pp. 368–9): 'So that as God has hitherto, instead of an Eternal Spring, a standing Serenity, and perpetual Sun-shine, subjected Mankind to the dismal influence of Comets from above, to Thunder, and Lightning, and Tempests from the middle Region, and from the lower Surface, to the raging of the Seas, and the tottering of Earth-quakes, beside all other the innumerable calamities to which humane life is exposed...' This was the England of 1673.

seemed to need some external object, some grit round which his pearl could form; the poems crystallize round Dew or Tears or the Bermudas. The poetry is neither doctrinal nor devotional. Marvell does not share Herbert's attitude to the Deity as a Person; or if he did, his writing is not informed by it. There is no direct appeal, no sense of *Deus Incarnatus*. On the other hand, while the attitude implied in such a poem as *The Coronet* could hardly subsist without dogma, dogma does not enter into it as it stands. The poem is about repentence, but it is repentence for the inevitable failings of human nature, the inability to get motives clear or feelings pure, a theme which in itself would not be foreign to the nineteenth century, as for instance it is represented at its best by Matthew Arnold.[1] Yet since Arnold generally felt unhappy but not guilty, because not responsible, he could never have achieved the powerful effect implicit in Marvell's grave, slow 'turn' from the opening rhythmic complexities, the weaving of the coronet, to the simplicity of its rejection:

> And now when I have summ'd up all my store,
> > Thinking (so I my self deceive)
> > So rich a Chaplet thence to weave
> As never yet the king of Glory wore:
> > Alas I find the Serpent old
> > That, twining in his speckled breast,
> > About the flow'rs disguis'd does fold,
> > With wreaths of Fame and Interest.

[1] The difference can be seen from e.g. *A Summer Night* and *The Future*. Arnold contemplates the impurity as a result of the age he lives in, as peculiar and temporary (*Dover Beach*) and therefore as a misfortune, not part of Original Sin.

This is perhaps of all Marvell's poems the most 'simple, sensuous, and passionate'. The complex structure is not obtrusive because Marvell was used to the complex and could take it for granted, 'Though set with Skill and chosen out with Care'.

This structure is a matter of rhythm and rhyme: the complicated plaiting of octosyllabic and decasyllabic, and the elaborate intertwining of the rhyme scheme represent both the coronet and the serpent: but it is the weighted cadences of the verse which carry the conviction of personal sincerity that makes the poem so impressive.[1] It is natural that Marvell should treat such a theme implicitly rather than explicitly, and the rather flat metaphor of the coronet, together with the plain vocabulary, strengthen the reserve and the self-control which are an essential part of this kind of religious humility. They are at the core of the Puritan tradition, as represented by Bunyan's Mr Valiant, and the Christ of *Paradise Regained*:

> But thou who only could'st the Serpent tame,
> Either his slipp'ry knots at once untie,
> And disintangle all his winding Snare:
> Or shatter too with him my curious frame:
> And let these wither, so that he may die.[2]

On a Drop of Dew is very similar, and deals with a similar feeling, but it is less personal and therefore more explicit. The dew, scarcely touching the flower,

---

[1] It is noticeable that only in his religious poetry does Marvell use any great variety of rhyme scheme and any complicated stanza forms.

[2] The cluttered consonants of the second line trailing into the sibilants of the third may be admired simply as a *tour de force*, though they are hardly noticed in ordinary reading.

> . . . gazing back upon the Skies,
> Shines with a mournful Light;
> Like its own Tear, . . .

and the Soul, too, 'Shuns the sweat leaves and blossoms green' and looks back to Heaven. The light, but constantly varying rhythm, and the braiding of rhymes again reflect the meaning which touches nowhere for long: the mind, like the dewdrop, is kept in a very delicate state of balance.[1] But the poem is not personal, and is less intense than *The Coronet*. The neatness of the simile and the emblematic character of dew[2] give a more self-contained interest to the descriptive parts of the poem, and indeed the 'sweat leaves and blossoms green', though repudiated, seem just as pure and almost as ethereal as the dewdrop, so that the poem is paradoxical in that the simile contradicts what it professes to assert about Nature and Heaven being distinct. The conflict is simpler because it is given in a scene; whereas in *The Coronet* and *A Dialogue between the Soul and Body* the problem is entirely that of 'this little world of man'.

This dialogue deals with a philosophical rather than a religious conflict but modified in such a way that conflict is hardly an appropriate term. The poem is a dialogue in the sense of a *duet* much more than a *debate*. Neither the Soul nor the Body is given pre-eminence; and though each protests against the limitations imposed by union with the other, yet

---

[1] Cf. W. Empson, *Seven Types of Ambiguity*, p. 100.

[2] E.g. Shakespeare, *Midsummer Night's Dream*, 4. 1. 57–60; Herrick, *To Dewes*, a song; *To Primroses filled with Morning Dew*; *To Daffodills*; *The Primrose*; Marvell, *Eyes and Tears*, l. 28.

neither can recognize a really independent existence. The Soul speaks in metaphors from bodily sensations:

> I feel, that cannot feel, the pain.

And the Body has no consciousness of itself except through the Soul, which

> Has made me live to let me dye.

Man is the unhappiest part of creation, since he alone is at once an animal and divine.

But beside the mutual thwarting of the soul and body, which is the ostensible subject of the poem as it is of *On a Drop of Dew*, their unity inflicts a deeper pain; soul and body suffer jointly the inescapable limitations of humanity. The Body's last words show it:

> So Architects do square and hew,
> Green Trees that in the Forest grew.

An architect destroys the natural beauty of the green trees; he creates a new beauty, but both kinds are incomplete. It is the steady recognition and acceptance of this incompleteness, underlying the opposition of body and soul, which makes the poem so moving and so unusual for its time. Few of Marvell's contemporaries would have recognized the claims of the Body as equal with those of the Soul. All the Soul's emotions appear as diseases to the Body, and it is the Soul which leads man into sin; the Body is naturally good. Every part of man feels its dual life: the heart is 'double' not only in Harvey's sense of having double ventricles; being the heart of a man it is also 'deceitful above all things'. The body is necessarily informed with soul, the soul is completely embedded in flesh.[1]

This parallel status of mind and matter was, as we have said, quite untypical of the age, but it can be traced throughout all the poems which have been considered in this chapter. Marvell could well afford to despise the vogue for Hobbes because he had always given matter a full recognition. Even in his most Puritanical and ascetic poem, he contrives by suggestion to include a good deal of his opponent's case in his own plea.

A Dialogue between the Resolved Soul, and Created Pleasure shows the soul completely in control of the situation and assisted by the body. The gaiety and flourishes are a celebration of that fact; the whole poem is much less serious in its total effect. The soul may begin with a reminiscence of St Paul,[2] but the body joins in with a muscular resilience which suggests equally swordsmanship and dancing:

> Courage my Soul, now learn to wield
> The weight of thine immortal Shield.
> Close on thy Head thy Helmet bright.
> Ballance thy Sword against the Fight.

(*Ballance* was used chiefly of poise in dancing, walking the tight rope, and fencing. Marvell had learnt fencing in Spain where the best masters were found.) The

---

[1] Here again there is a fugitive likeness to Spinoza. For his statements on the equality of the two modes of Thought and Extension see *Ethics*, II. Props. 1–4, 7, and v. 1. See also Appendix C.

[2] *To the Ephesians*, VI. 16–17. 'Above all, taking the shielde of Faith, wherewith yee shall bee able to quench all the fierie dartes of the wicked. And take the helmet of salvation, and the Sword of the Spirit, which is the word of God.' The order of weapons is the same.

'Army, strong as fair', is repulsed with a liveliness which suggests anything but asceticism; almost with the gallantry of the courtly poems. At the same time the Soul's replies are fuller and more inclusive than the charges of Pleasure:

Pleasure. On these downy Pillows lye,
Whose soft Plumes will thither fly:
On these Roses strow'd so plain
Lest one Leaf thy Side should strain.

Soul. My gentler Rest is on a Thought,
Conscious of doing what I ought.

The reply itself is gentle: but *rest* includes the idea not only of *repose* but of *choice* (as in the final speech of Romeo); and also more remotely that of *support*, e.g. the iron *rest* on which the musketeer leaned his barrel. This paradoxical firmness in the idea of *gentler rest*, the underlying iron fixity, steady as the iron wedges of Fate, confirms, without making too fierce, the resolution of the Soul. In the same way the pun on music,

Cease Tempter. None can chain a mind
Whom this sweet Chordage cannot bind,

is paradoxical, since chords are weaker than chains,[1] and the clash of the *Cease Tempter* sounds more like the snapping of links than strands parting. Immediately after this rejection of music, the very musical chorus bursts into operatic celebration:

Then persevere: for still new Charges sound:
And if thou overcom'st thou shalt be crown'd.

[1] This point was made by W. Empson, *op. cit.* pp. 134–5: and there is also an analysis by F. R. Leavis (*Revaluations*, Chatto and Windus, 1937, pp. 26–7) which makes a comparison with Dryden.

F

As the combat grows sharper and victory more certain, the rejection of Beauty, Wealth, Power and Knowledge is much more epigrammatic than the repulse of the five senses. But the last reply deflects the result:

> None thither mounts by the degree
> Of Knowledge, but Humility.

The Chorus immediately breaks into the final paean:

> *Triumph, triumph, victorious Soul....*

The conflict in this poem is not very serious: the variety and perseverance of the charges only add to the glories of the immutably resolved soul. It is a public affair, and with its puns and its gallantry seems to belong to the Nunappleton period. Yet 'the eagles and the trumpets' have the sanction of the true Miltonic sublime. Marvell could not have used a style so operatic to achieve results so different from Dryden's if he had not also been capable of the very different writing of *The Coronet*.

Marvell's political poetry in its development supports the conjectured progression of his other work: first there is *An Horatian Ode*, which corresponds in the balanced antinomies of thought and feeling, in verbal agility, to the period of *To his Coy Mistress*. Then the poems to Fairfax introduce a fuller, softer and more richly implicated style, which is encouraged by the more personal nature of the panegyric; but in the later political poems this style is transferred to more public and impersonal subjects.

An Horatian Ode, though probably the most famous of Marvell's poems, has more often been judged by the parts rather than by the whole. Like *To his Coy Mistress*, it has a triple movement, the Hegelian thesis, antithesis and synthesis. The thesis is the impersonal power of Cromwell:

> 'Tis Madness to resist or blame
> The force of angry Heavens flame.

The antithesis is the personal dignity and comeliness of Charles, which may offset Cromwell's achievement: and the synthesis is the acceptance of Cromwell, both his 'forced Pow'r' and his personal unattractiveness, because he puts England first:

> And has his Sword and Spoyls ungirt,
> To lay them at the *Publick's* skirt.

The transitions amount to reversals here, and the poem may well represent the steps of reasoning by which the friend of Lovelace threw in his lot with the Roundheads: it is only after this date that we hear of Marvell being as definitely on their side. The attitude of this poem is substantially that of *The Rehearsal Transpros'd*, written more than twenty years later,[1] when Marvell was practising in adversity the same principles of toleration which he illustrated in the hour of success.

There is a farewell to love poetry in the opening lines, which are pleasantly ironic, seeing that Marvell was just about to write his best love poems:

[1] See Chapter IV, p. 93.

> The forward Youth that would appear
> Must now forsake his *Muses* dear.[1]

Cromwell, the man of destiny, is shown not only following but urging his 'active Star'; he is impelled, but also adds his own force, and the result is a kind of Caesarean birth in more senses than one, where both he and his own Star will each

> thorough his own Side
> His fiery way divide.

The ensuing destruction was a natural process: within a given spot there can be only one object at one time:

> Nature that hateth emptiness,
> Allows of penetration less:
>   And therefore must make room
>   Where greater Spirits come.

Then, for the antithesis, we are given Charles, the hunted lion, caught by a toil: but although this is partly a proof of Cromwell's 'wiser Art', the paradoxes and puns by which it is stated make the process more complicated and therefore less villainous; sympathy for Charles is not hatred of Cromwell:

> Where, twining subtile fears with hope,
> He wove a Net of such a scope,
>   That *Charles* himself might chase
>   To *Caresbrooks* narrow case.[2]

The series of puns on the Tragic Scaffold turn the execution into a public impersonal act while retaining

---

[1] *Forward* means both *precocious* and *brave* and attracts *appear* into a rather more concrete sense than it would normally bear: the march begins. Marvell himself was something more than a forward youth in 1650, being then nine-and-twenty.

[2] *Subtile* and *case* are used in both abstract and concrete senses: a *net of scope* is paradoxical, *himself* either nominative or accusative.

all the pathos of the Royal Actor's humanity: the soldiers sympathetically applaud Charles, the tragic hero:

> While round the armed Bands
> Did clap their bloody hands.[1]

Personal heroism is allowed full scope: in the description of Charles bowing his comely head, Cromwell is weighed—Cromwell, with his rough manners, his lack of any personal attractiveness.

Having set all this forth, the synthesis emerges. It is neither Charles, nor Cromwell, but England, the 'Capitol', the 'Republick', the 'Isle', which is the pivot of the poem. Cromwell can 'obey': he is the falcon, but England is the falconer, and the victory that plumes his crest is a triumph of civilization as well as of force. The pun on the 'sad' valour of the Roundheads implies that a civilized state can digest 'the forced Pow'r'; the sword which Cromwell holds erect is efficacious against the 'Spirits of the shady Night' by the cross on the hilt and against more mundane terrors by the power of the blade. The poem celebrates no triumph of expediency: the full recognition of

> Though Justice against Fate complain,...
> This was that memorable Hour
> Which first assur'd the forced Pow'r...
>   The same *Arts* that did *gain*
>   A *Pow'r* must it *maintain*....

provides a measure of Cromwell's acts but not of their

---

[1] Harrington, Marvell's intimate friend, was one of the two or three persons actually present on the scaffold. The passage may owe something to him. (See Aubrey, *Brief Lives*, ed. cit. vol. I, pp. 288–9; and Harrington, *Works*, ed. Toland (1771), p. xiv.)

motives nor of their results. The first belong to 'angry Heaven', the last to England. Cromwell is God's instrument and the Commons' servant. If the poem may seem to leave the realm of strict fact (particularly in the Irish tribute—'They can affirm his Praises best') that does not invalidate it nor make the range of sympathies less.

The Nunappleton poems have neither the tension nor the strength of *An Horatian Ode*, and Fairfax is seen not as the saviour of England, but as the lord of a Yorkshire manor. Yet his relation to the scene in *Upon the Hill and Grove at Bill-borow* is much the same as Cromwell's relation to England. Marvell identifies 'The *Genius* of the house' with the trees which 'in their *Lord's* advancement grow', yet he stops also for a descriptive aside telling how the 'fluttring Breez'

> Discourses with the breathing Trees;
> Which in their modest Whispers name
> Those Acts that swell'd the Cheek of Fame.

The landscape is not being made an illustration of Fairfax's modesty: it exists in its own right. In *Musicks Empire* the continuity between the human, the inanimate, the political and the religious aspects of the ceremony is still more complete. Marvell can be seen evolving his own sense of 'The wondrous Architecture of the world'; something other than a theoretical conception, and yet something articulated rather than a purely instinctive or intuitive feeling.

Music is related to the Ptolemaic harmonies and so to the creation of the world:

> First was the World as one great Cymbal made,

but it was man, building and colonizing the 'Organs City', who led the 'solitary sound' of Nature first to an earthly and then to a heavenly power:

> Victorious sounds! yet here your Homage do
> Unto a gentler Conqueror then you;
> Who, though He flies the Musick of his praise,
> Would with you Heavens Hallelujahs raise.

The music of the spheres therefore remains the symbol of the earthly music, of the military triumphs of Fairfax and of the religious purposes for which those triumphs were won. The compliment is both placed and enhanced by the grandeur and gallantry of its setting, and the variety of elements resolved in this poem is not a variety within a single kind (as it is in *Alexander's Feast*, for example),[1] yet the process appears single and spontaneous.

The poems to Fairfax were, however, as much personal as political poems. In the panegyrics which Marvell wrote later there is little personal feeling. Only *The First Anniversary* came out at the time that it was written; it is the most typical, as well as the most important poem of this group. In it Marvell combines the richness of the poems to Lord Fairfax with something of the nervous power of *An Horatian Ode*:

[1] Mark van Doren (*The Poetry of John Dryden*, Harcourt Brace, 1920, pp. 253–4) compares these two poems in Dryden's favour: 'Marvell has only hinted at the possibilities that lie in the figure of Jubal and the -ell rhymes while Dryden has extracted the utmost whether of drama or of sound from both.' But Marvell was not concerned to produce a technical *tour de force* or even 'vitality and good nature on the grand scale'.

Like the vain Curlings of the Watry maze,
Which in smooth streams a sinking Weight does raise;
So Man, declining alwayes, disappears
In the weak Circles of increasing Years;
And his short Tumults of themselves Compose,
While flowing Time above his Head does close.[1]

This begins as a simile but with the 'weak Circles of
increasing Years' it has become metaphor, and suggests
also the circling of the planets, of which the oldest have
the largest circles. The antitheses 'sinking...raise'
and 'weak...increasing' seem to make the process of
decay partly compensatory and not merely melan-
choly; and Time 'closes' above man's head not only
like Watts' ever-rolling stream but also like a 'close'
in music.

Such an opening not only disposes of Charles I,
perhaps, and Marvell's own early sympathies, it also
reminds the reader that although this is a panegyric,
the poet remembers the scale to which he is working:
what he is about to say may sound absolute, but
this is a reminder that it is only relative after all. He
passes on to a dozen lines of wit and satire, in which,
the planetary metaphor now dominant, the Sun-like
Cromwell is compared with 'heavy Monarchs...more
Malignant then *Saturn*'.[2] Cromwell as the Sun, the
animating principle of Nature, is the central image of
the poem; it is the kind of identification of human and
natural forces that has been already seen in the poems
to Fairfax.[3] This anniversary is a cosmic event, and,

[1] ll. 1–6.
[2] Malignant in a planetary and political sense.
[3] Kings on the contrary are mechanic timepieces: '(Image-like) an

tuned with the Ptolemaic harmonies, Cromwell's progress is also an ascension:

> While indefatigable *Cromwell* hyes,
> And cuts his way still nearer to the Skyes,
> Learning a Musique in the Region clear,
> To tune this lower to that higher Sphere.[1]

It is perhaps as Apollo or at least as Phaethon that he appears in the passage where Marvell contrives in the grand heroic manner a description of the one calamity of the year, when Cromwell upset his own coach in Hyde Park and spilt himself badly. This was a punishment for the sins of the nation at large:

> Our brutish fury strugling to be Free,
> Hurry'd thy Horses while they hurry'd thee....
> Thou *Cromwell* falling, not a stupid Tree,
> Or Rock so savage, but it mourn'd for thee:
> And all about was heard a Panique groan,
> As if that Natures self were overthrown.
> It seem'd the Earth did from the Center tear;
> It seem'd the Sun was faln out of the Sphere:
> Justice obstructed lay, and Reason fool'd;
> Courage disheartned, and Religion cool'd.[2]

The repetition is the first break in the rhythmic gravity; but if the last four personifications stand for Cromwell as the Sun does, the verbs are impolite enough, and the last suggests a sousing.[3]

This catastrophe fills all the central part of the

---

useless time they tell And with vain Scepter, strike the hourly Bell.'
Cf. the contrast of natural and mechanical time in *The Garden*.

   [1] ll. 45–8.   [2] ll. 177–8, 201–8.

   [3] The passage recalls Virgil on the death of Julius Cæsar in the fifth *Eclogue*. The rhythm and tone, the measured and ponderous emphasis suggest the stately progress that should have been Cromwell's but was not: this leaves the pomp of the vocabulary undiluted.

poem, where the sins of the nations are enumerated in the sins of Levellers and Fifth Monarchy Men; but in the emergence of the sunlike Cromwell, it is his followers who are ridiculed. The passage is grand in a moving way at first, as it describes exploration at sunrise in the early world:

> So when first Man did through the Morning new
> See the bright Sun his shining Race pursue,
> All day he follow'd with unwearied sight,
> Pleas'd with that other World of moving Light.[1]

This American dawn is put fairly flatly against the poetical trappings with which the preposterous savage mourns what he thinks is the final extinction of the Sun at sunset, till at the end of a pathetic outburst,

> ...streight the Sun behind him he descry'd
> Smiling serenely from the further side.[2]

The best panegyric has often an element of satire, as the best satire has an element of panegyric. This anticipates possible objections, forestalls criticism and intensifies by contrast the main purpose of the work.[3]

Cromwell has been shown in almost godlike control of the political order, so that this interlude is really called for. In the earlier part of the poem he is shown building the Commonwealth by divine power, as Amphion built the walls of Thebes with music. Amphion and Orpheus were old and familiar symbols for the great man's godlike control over Nature; and

---

[1] ll. 325–8.   [2] ll. 341–2.
[3] Dryden's *Absalom and Achitophel* is the classic instance.

in both instances the control is by means of music, by again invoking those Ptolemaic harmonies which are the foundations of the world. The Heavenly music is so potent that

> The rougher Stones, unto his Measures hew'd,
> Dans'd up in order from the Quarreys rude.[1]

The Parliamentary terms, *Measure* and *order*, lead up to the most audacious pun, that on Cromwell tuning the Ruling Instrument, i.e. the Instrument of Government; they give an immense feeling of gaiety and success.

As in *Musicks Empire*, the different colonies have different functions:

> Now through the Strings a Martial rage he throws,
> And joyning streight the *Theban* Tow'r arose;
> Then as he strokes them with a Touch more sweet,
> The flocking Marbles in a Palace meet.[2]

Even the disagreements of his followers are used to advantage:

> While the resistance of opposed Minds,
> The Fabrick as with Arches stronger binds,
> Which on the Basis of a Senate free,
> Knit by the Roofs Protecting weight agree.[3]

The 'Protecting weight' in this case might seem of much more importance than the basis provided by the Rump Parliament; but it has already been made clear that this is a panegyric and that consistency is more important than veracity. Cromwell's methods are again those of Heaven itself, for the Opposition

[1] ll. 51–2.   [2] ll. 59–62.   [3] ll. 95–8.

is part of the divine plan to put off the Day of Judgment:

> Hence that blest Day still counterpoysed wastes,
> The Ill delaying, what th'Elected hastes.[1]

How far Marvell's sense of humour was appreciated by those for whom he wrote it is rather difficult to decide. His letter to Cromwell might almost be taken as a parody, so perfectly has he caught the unctuous tone of psalmodic Dissent; but one cannot assume that he would take such liberties with the great man. His power of mimicry and unconscious adaptation was considerable: it was to be one of the weapons of his satire under Charles II.

A Poem upon the Death of O. C.[2] employs the same combination of images as *The First Anniversary*, but the result is unimpressive. In contrast, in *An Epitaph upon*—, 'Enough, and leave the rest to Fame', the keenness of grief rejecting comment and the control almost unconsciously cutting it short concur in that measured brevity which both demand. The need to write at length defeated him. The passage on the dead Cromwell, detached, has power:

> I saw him dead...
> Yet dwelt that greatnesse in his shape decay'd,
> That still though dead, greater than death he lay'd;
> And in his alter'd face you something faigne
> That threatens death, he yet will live again.[3]

A poem on death does not allow any great variety of tone: the available evidence does not suggest that Marvell had any affection for Cromwell the man, as

---

[1] ll. 155–6.   [2] He died 3 September 1658.   [3] ll. 247 ff.

he obviously had for Fairfax. He has no personal feeling to nourish the conception that Cromwell died of grief at his daughter's death, and it becomes merely an ingenious conceit, designed to glorify a death otherwise rather too placid for a hero.

The impression of patchwork is strengthened by the very large number of borrowings from Virgil, particularly from the *Georgics*, which as they are used here are not often worth the carriage.[1]

The poem serves to show how little Marvell was at home in a situation which would not have found Waller, Cowley or Dryden at a loss. The public occasion as such did not arouse him: for his conception of the State as part of the natural order required to be infused somewhere by personal feeling. The same thing remains true of his later prose writings also, for he only joined battle where his friends were involved already.

Marvell's political theory derived largely from his friend Harrington, on whose *Oceana* he was later to draw freely. Harrington's treatise combines a penetrating account of the contemporary economic situation, and an economic interpretation of history (which has led to his being called the first Marxist), with a good deal of naïve panegyric of Olphaeus Megalator,

---

[1] *A Poem upon the Death of O. C.* ll. 101–32, cf. *Georgics*, 1, 463 ff.; ll. 123–6, cf. Ovid, *Met.* VII, 542–4 and *Georgics*, 3, 522–4; ll. 261–2, cf. *Georgics*, 2, 291–2; ll. 281–6, cf. *Eclogues*, 5, 76–8; ll. 117–18, cf. *Georgics*, 1, 316–21; ll. 121–2, cf. *Georgics*, 1, 321–7; ll. 113–16, cf. *Georgics*, 1, 328–34. In *The First Anniversary* there are comparatively few echoes: l. 46, cf. *Georgics*, 4, 561; ll. 191–205, cf. *Eclogues*, 5, 20–8 and *Georgics*, 1, 479; l. 197, cf. *Georgics*, 1, 375.

the Saviour of the Commonwealth. On one page he will tackle the question of land tenure with comprehensiveness and on the next suggest that the solution of the Irish question is to plant the island with Jews, since they are the only race with sufficient energy to withstand the effects of the relaxing climate.

But Harrington, like Marvell, could unite the most discrepant material because he felt the continuity of the natural and the social order; because he kept the old Elizabethan conception of the body politic, which was very different from Hobbes' new theory of the state as a contract, a piece of cosmic business:

O the most blest and fortunat of all countrys, OCEANA! how deservedly has Nature with the bountys of heaven and earth indu'd thee? thy ever fruitful womb not clos'd with ice, nor dissolv'd by the raging star: where *Ceres* and *Bacchus* are perpetual twins. Thy woods are not the harbor of devouring beasts, nor thy continual verdure the ambush of serpents, but the food of innumerable herds and flocks presenting thee their shepherdess with distended dugs, or golden fleeces. The wings of thy night involve thee not in the horror of darkness, but have still som white feather: and thy day is (that for which we esteem life) the longest.[1]

Such a view had been Marvell's: but after the Restoration, external circumstances no longer endorsed it, and Marvell's political poetry is of little interest. The many pieces of doggerel which he turned out were 'writ well to the purpose he intended', but that was not a poetic purpose. It is only necessary to compare the picture of Amphion in *Clarindon's*

[1] Harrington, *Works*, ed. cit. p. 32 (translating Pliny).

House-Warming with the one which has been quoted from *The First Anniversary* to see how much the Restoration had killed.[1]

Only one of the later satires has any claims to be called poetry, and that is *The last Instructions to a Painter*. It is like the prose of this period in being controversial. Waller had written a serious panegyric, *Instructions to a Painter*, which was parodied by the Opposition: Marvell's is one of five such parodies.[2]

The poem belongs to 1667, and satirically describes the meeting of Parliament and a debate over the Excise, with an account of the Dutch naval triumphs at Sheerness and Chatham, the death of Captain Douglas in the naval battle, and a final vision of the King.

These pictures or pageants which compose it are reminiscent of Marvell's earliest emblematic style, but the vocabulary is much more colloquial. There is a crispness about the language and a savage emphasis in the rhythm that make the burlesque alive. For example, the incompetence of the Navy is satirically set against the mock-battle over the Excise:[3] this is the

---

[1] See p. 79 above. And cf. the satiric description of the conspiracy between Louis XIV and the Court Party in 1677: 'for all things... moved with that punctual Regularity that it was like the Harmony of the Spheres, so Consonant with themselves, although we cannot hear the musick' (Grosart, *Works*, Vol. IV, p. 374).

[2] The series was evidently famous and set a wide-spread fashion. Dr Johnson mentions it in *The Rambler*, No. 121.

[3] In *The First Anniversary* (ll. 355-62) the English Navy is an unassailable force of Nature, and the poem *On the Victory obtained by Blake* celebrates it at greater length. Marvell, as a Hull man, was naturally interested in naval matters.

only kind of warfare at which the English are skilled.
The debate is described in terms of an engagement:

> Of early Wittals first the Troop march'd in,
> For Diligence renown'd, and Discipline:
> In Loyal haste they left young Wives in Bed,
> And *Denham* these by one consent did head.[1]

Traitors, Cowards, Court Officers, Bishops, Lawyers,
and others follow. These pursue a policy for which
they were to upbraid the Dutch and attack in a time
of truce:

> Thick was the Morning, and the *House* was thin,
> The *Speaker* early, when they all fell in.[2]

In spite of this advantage, they are routed by a troup
of 'Presbyterian Switzers' and a 'Gross of English
Gentry'. The rejoicings are abruptly stopped, however, by the real war. The Dutch are sailing up the
Thames in idyllic peacefulness:

> So have I seen in *April*'s bud, arise
> A Fleet of Clouds, sailing along the Skies:
> The liquid Region with their Squadrons fill'd,
> The airy Sterns the Sun behind does guild;
> And gentle Gales them steer, and Heaven drives.[3]

It is horribly ironic (and perhaps more ironic than
he meant it to be) that Marvell should only regain the
mood of Virgilian grace in describing the action
which was such a shame to the country. De Ruyter
is now the happy conqueror ('His sporting Navy all
about him swim') while the English are constrained
to stop the passage by sinking their own ships: those
which had brought

[1] ll. 151–4.   [2] ll. 235–6.   [3] ll. 551 ff.

From *Gambo* Gold, and from the *Ganges* Gems;
Take a short Voyage underneath the *Thames*.[1]

The only consolation is the valiant death of Captain Douglas, who was burnt on his ship, refusing to surrender, or to leave without orders. This is the part of the poem that Marvell later put into the mouth of Cleveland: and in fact there is a good deal of Clevelandism in it,[2]—of that decorative elaboration of the conceit which reduced the most violently passionate situations to the formality and weight of tapestry. The young man in the midst of the fire is not a human figure at all and we are not allowed any human feelings about him:

> His shape exact, which the bright flames infold,
> Like the Sun's Statue stands of burnish'd Gold.
> Round the transparent Fire about him glows,
> As the clear Amber on the Bee does close:
> And, as on Angels Heads their Glories shine,
> His burning Locks adorn his Face Divine.[3]

It is not on Douglas only that the 'clear Amber' has closed. The sensuous beauty of this description has nothing of ordinary life: heroes can still be recognized, but not recognized for human, as were Cromwell and Fairfax. If there was irony in the author of *Upon Appleton House* finding something of his old material in describing De Ruyter's advance, there is equal irony in this petrifying praise. Douglas, silhouetted in fire, is as it were the embalmed body of patriotism; something shining and far off, like the Miltonic Messiah.

[1] ll. 719–20.
[2] Marvell used this part of the poem for a piece called *The Loyall Scot* which he put into the mouth of Cleveland as a sort of palinode for *The Rebel Scot*.   [3] ll. 679–84.

G

The final pageant, that of Charles himself, is in the grand manner, yet it manages to combine outraged patriotism with stinging personal satire. Charles has a vision of England—which he confounds with a vision of one of his mistresses. But it is a real vision of that England which died at the Restoration, and which remained to Marvell, as it here appears to Charles, as something unsubstantial, a ghost:

> Paint last the King, and a dead shade of Night,
> Only dispers'd by a weak Tapers light;
> And those bright gleams that dart along and glare
> From his clear Eyes, yet these too dark with Care.
> There, as in the calm horrour all alone,
> He wakes and Muses of th'uneasie Throne:
> Raise up a sudden Shape with Virgins Face,
> Though ill agree her Posture, Hour or Place....
>
> The Object strange in him no Terrour mov'd:
> He wonder'd first, then pity'd, then he lov'd:
> And with kind hand does the coy Vision press,
> Whose Beauty greater seem'd by her distress;
> But soon shrunk back, chill'd with her touch so cold,
> And th'airy Picture vanisht from his hold.
> In his deep thoughts the wonder did increase,
> And he Divin'd 'twas *England* or the *Peace*.[1]

Here Marvell's quiet grave tone and his power of weighting the lines with implication recall something of the old manner, and the vivid vision of the murdered Charles I which follows, when the ghost comes to warn his son, shows by its macabre contrast how far Marvell is from the world of *An Horatian Ode* :[2]

[1] ll. 885 ff.

[2] Perhaps there is a reminiscence of this poem in the lines quoted above, however. Cf. the first line, and the last verse of *An Horatian Ode*.

> Shake then the room, and all his Curtains tear,
> And with blue streaks infect the Taper clear:...
> And ghastly *Charles*, turning his Collar low,
> The purple thread about his Neck does show.[1]

This poem has also in places the merits of an insolence more assured than that of the Cavaliers, as in the description of Jermyn—

> Paint then St. *Albans* full of soup and gold,
> The new *Courts* pattern, Stallion of the old—

and in the polished innuendo by which Marvell apologizes for advising the King, while reminding him maliciously that things have not always been as now:

> Kings in the Country oft have gone astray,
> Nor of a Peasant scorn'd to learn the way.[2]

Once, in an attempt at the old unity, he declares,

> (But *Ceres* Corn, and *Flora* is the Spring,
> *Bacchus* is Wine, the Country is the *King*.)[3]

But here the touchingly flat statement sounds as if it describes what ought to be, not what is. Perception has frozen into mythology.

These flashes do not make a poem; and the co-ordinating power behind Marvell's greater work, which was more than a personal power, had departed. He could retire into the country 'some five miles of to injoy the spring & my privacy',[4] or he could risk the pillory with a pamphlet; he could no longer write poetry. This was the age of Dryden, whom Marvell did not like. Three years only after Marvell's death appeared the first part of *Absalom and Achitophel*.

---

[1] ll. 915 ff.   [2] ll. 959–60.   [3] ll. 973–4.
[4] Margoliouth, *Misc. Letters*, No. 18.

IV

'THE REHEARSAL TRANSPROS'D'

All Marvell's pamphlets and, with one or two exceptions, his extant letters belong to the last twenty years of his life (1658–78),—the pamphlets to the last six years. There is, therefore, a gap of fourteen years between the period when it is supposed that he wrote his best lyrics (i.e. before 1658), and the period when he became famous as a writer of pamphlets. In the course of these twenty years Marvell was Assistant in the Office of the Foreign Secretary, and Member for Hull.

The prose consists of letters to the mayor and burgesses of Hull, the Brethren of the Trinity House, and a few to friends and relatives, with four pamphlets of undoubted authenticity, three of which are parts of religious controversies (*The Rehearsal Transpros'd*, 1672–3; *Mr Smirke*, 1676; *Remarks upon a Late Disingenuous Discourse*, 1678), while the fourth is a religio-political tract, *An Account of the Growth of Popery and Arbitrary Government in England*, 1677.

The Rehearsal Transpros'd took its title from the Duke of Buckingham's farce,[1] and was the literary sensation of its time. Mr Bayes, the hero, signified Samuel Parker, Archdeacon of Canterbury and future

[1] Buckingham's brother, Francis Villiers, had been the subject of an elegy by Marvell: and the Duke had married Mary Fairfax, though at this time he neglected her shockingly.

Bishop of Oxford, who whilst advocating dictatorship by the state in religion, had attacked the Declaration of Indulgence. He was answered by John Owen, and replied to Owen in a Preface to one of the works of Bishop Bramhall which he edited for the occasion: in this he attacked not only Owen, but Richard Baxter and Milton. Marvell wrote *The Rehearsal Transpros'd* in answer to Parker's whole case, and when Parker administered a *Reproof* he replied with a Second Part. Parker was a time-server and a bully: it was he whom James II later forcibly installed as President of Magdalen.

In the brush with Marvell he had the worst of it. Burnet spoke of the poet as

the liveliest droll of the age, who writ in a burlesque strain, but with so peculiar and entertaining a conduct, that from the king down to the tradesman his book was read with great pleasure. That not only humbled Parker, but the whole party: for the author of the Rehearsal Transprosed had all the men of wit (or, as the French phrase it, all the *laughers*) of his side.[1]

The First Part of *The Rehearsal Transpros'd* at first sight appears rather repetitive and discursive, but only because Marvell is answering three different books of Parker:

1. *A Discourse of Ecclesiastical Policy*, 1670. (Answered in *The Rehearsal Transpros'd*, pp. 1–70 of Grosart's edition, *Works*, vol. III.)

2. *A Defense of the Ecclesiastical Policy*, in a Letter to the Author of the *Friendly Debate*, 1671. (Answered, *ibid.* pp. 70–99.)

[1] *History of My Own Times*, ed. Airy, vol. I, pp. 467–8.

3. *A Preface*, showing what grounds there are for fears and jealousies of Popery, prefixed to the *Vindication* of Bishop Bramhall, 1672. (Answered, *ibid.* pp. 185 ff.)

The answer to *Ecclesiastical Policy* is the kernel of the case. Each book is dealt with under several heads, analytic of the argument. There is comparatively little personal matter except an occasional reference to Owen.

The Second Part of *The Rehearsal Transpros'd* is different. Marvell was here replying to gross personal attacks from Parker and half a dozen pamphleteers, some of whose charges have been mentioned in Chapter 1. Parker's book is, however, the only one he notes at length. Here Marvell becomes personal in turn, and relies much less on argument: for he had not really a case to answer now; his only need was to silence his opponents' scurrilities. There is an apology for himself, a lengthy genealogy and history of Parker and a general recapitulation before he settles down to answering the new book in formal style, which he does under six heads or 'acts' of the play.[1] He concludes with refuting some of the attacks on his friends, particularly those on Milton and John Hales; and there is a clinching quotation from Bacon. There is a good deal of pure raillery in the Second Part; but at the beginning Marvell makes some very spirited statements of his views on Church and State.

It is at first sight a useless task to rake up dead ecclesiastical controversy about points of practice long since decided. But in considering Marvell's

[1] Grosart, *loc. cit.* pp. 325–460.

part in these discussions, several factors of permanent importance emerge. First, the underlying principles which prompted him, which were much more general than those of the controversy. The idea of toleration, that every man should be free in matters of conscience and ritual, was one which was just coming to birth after the painful struggle which had lasted since the Reformation. Here and there in a single mind we may see it beginning to live. Marvell's was one of these minds.[1] Unlike Parker and his party, who used dissension as a means of advancement, he considered that the first duty of a Christian was to Christianity rather than to the Establishment.[2] Marvell's contribution was practical rather than theoretical: he affected public opinion, and so influenced the course of events. Something was added towards the solution of the problem of Dissent.

Secondly, Marvell's method was from the literary point of view something new. Pamphlet-wars had been common throughout the century, and some of the best prose, notably Milton's, had appeared in this way. Marvell's technique, however, was new. By his popular style, his free use of secular weapons, including the latest play, he pointed the way towards a more Augustan method of handling disputation. To

[1] Marvell's nephew, Will Popple, whose education he directed, was the first to translate from Latin Locke's *Letter on Toleration* (1689) and in a little book called *A Rational Catechism* (1687) he advocated toleration. Popple was also an intimate friend of Jean Le Clerc.

[2] The congruence between Church and State, is, of course, if the State is regarded as one of the ordinances of religion, more complicated than ever. See p. 117 n.

treat a grave subject lightly, yet with the serious intention of reinforcing the argument, was an art neglected since the Marprelates with whom Marvell is so often compared.

Marvell is shown not only as 'an incorruptible man in a corrupt age', but also as a religious man in an irreligious age. In addition, he is seen as a writer with the very nicest sense of the adaptation of means to ends. His immediate purpose is seen quite clearly as his ultimate purpose, and yet is kept distinct from it, which ambivalence meant a new use of detail, an enlistment of the finer points of writing more directly and particularly in the service of his cause.

The pamphlets have one common object: to assert the importance of the personal and spiritual side of religion against those who would not only emphasize externals, but whose lives and conduct had shown their interests to be worldly, who made a career out of the ministry and who were apparently unconscious of any wrong in jeering not only at the wilder habits of the unorthodox, but at any expression of feeling, however sincere and sacred, which was not entirely stereotyped. Parker laughed at Baxter's most personal religious confessions, on account of their enthusiastic language, which was after all no more enthusiastic than the subject might justify. Marvell was drawn to reply not only for the sake of the Nonconformists, but in defence of the finer principles of his own faith, which were outraged by such defenders. The violence of the clerical attack is that of an ecclesiastical *condottiere*, and the degree of tolerance Marvell advocated was

no less necessary for securing properly charitable and
disinterested Anglicanism than for the relieving of Dissenters. It was partly a reminder that unto Caesar
should be rendered the things that are Caesar's (and
so won the good word of Charles himself). Parker
would have wished to dominate the temporal power
as completely as a Boniface VIII: he would use it to
punish Nonconformity more severely than any temporal crime. Yet Nonconformity was the only spiritual
crime which he appeared to recognize; the seven
deadly sins would have been small matters in his
eye; of the cardinal virtues he seemed to admit only
prudence and fortitude as means to the fruits of the
spirit, improved upon in his own interpretation;
and as Marvell said, 'the Church of *England* is much
obliged to Mr. *Bayes* for having proved that Nonconformity is the Sin against the Holy Ghost'.[1]

The nature of his adversaries dictated the nature of
Marvell's reply. After Parker's treatment of Owen
and Baxter, there was nothing to be done by conduct-
ing the dispute upon a truly religious level. This
churchman had to be beaten on the only ground he
recognized: by demolishing his logical and historical
argument, and divesting him of his credit by making a
fool of him. Marvell, by his political and diplomatic
training, his personal wit, and his literary interests was
particularly well fitted for the work. Instead of being
faced with unworldly piety, intellectual simplicity
and unfashionable sobriety, Parker met with a cool,
skilful and sophisticated enemy, who had taken

[1] Grosart, *loc. cit.* p. 144.

his measure and that of his public. The Bible was little used in discussion with one who confounded grace and morality; he was set in his proper *milieu*, and wounded in matters he really cared about, by means of the latest comedy. An angry or serious defence only made him look more ridiculous: his one chance was to try to be witty, and on those grounds Marvell was pretty sure to win. He had in fact disarmed Parker.

The Archdeacon had taken it on himself to lay down very strictly the role of the temporal power in enforcing spiritual obedience, and of this part of his argument Marvell makes hay:

First therefore, as to the Power of the Magistrate he saith in gross: that *the Supream Government of every Common-wealth must of Necessity be Universal, Uncontrolable, Indispensible, Unlimited, and Absolute.*...if it be not Law, 'tis pity but it were so. 'Tis the very *Elixir Potestatis* and *Magisterium Domini:* So fine a thing that no man living but would be inamour'd with it: For, wot ye well, it is a *Power* he saith *established* of yore, at or before the beginning of the World, e're there was any such thing known or thought of, as Periwigs or Glass-Coaches....he lays his Imposition now upon the Magistrate, and leaves him not so much as the Power to will nor chuse; but he must govern by the Laws of the *Author of the Ecclesiastical Politie. He* must *scourge them into order. He* must *Chastise them out of their peevishness, and Lash them into Obedience,* (*Ec. Pol.* p. 325.)...Is this at last all the business why he hath been building up all this while that Necessary, Universal, Uncontroulable, Indispensible, Unlimited, Absolute Power of Governors; only to gratifie the humour and arrogance of an Unnecessary, Universal, Uncontroulable, Dispensible, Unlimited and Absolute, Arch-Deacon? Still *must, must, must:* But what if the Supream Magistrate won't?[1]   *R.T.* II, pp. 82–3, 88.

[1] Grosart, *loc. cit.* pp. 295, 300.

Parker's case was based on Hobbes' doctrine of the State, though applied to ends Hobbes would have disapproved. It was giving the monarchy absolute power, only to make it a more efficacious servant of the Church; and such a policy, as Marvell maliciously points out, was not at all agreeable to the Royalty in question:

But henceforward the King fell into disgrace with Mr. *Bayes*, and any one that had eyes might discern that our Author did not afford his Majesty that Countenance and Favour which he had formerly enjoy'd.[1]

R.T. i, pp. 136–7.

But though the Archdeacon might be laughed at for his principles of universal rule, his power to persecute was not small; and his intolerance was at least as fanatical as that of his opponents, and much less disinterested, in spite of his protest:

Now to lash these morose and churlish Zealots with smart and twingeing Satyrs is so farr from being a criminal Passion, that 'tis a zeal of Meekness and Charity, and a prosecution of the grand and diffusive duty of humanity, and proceeds only from an earnest desire to maintain the common Love and Charity of Mankind. And though Good manners oblige us to treat all other sorts of People with gentle and civil Language; yet when we have to do with the Scribes and Pharisees, we must point our Reproofs with sharp Invectives...[2]

The Archdeacon can be satirical about the doctrine of the Nonconformists in a way which implies very little respect for religion of any sort: Marvell quotes him:

'Put the case the Clergy were Cheats and Juglers, yet it must be allowed they are necessary Instruments of

---

[1] Grosart, *loc. cit.* p. 99.   [2] Preface to *Ecclesiastical Policy*, p. x.

State to aw the Common People into fear and obedience, because nothing else can so effectually inslave them' ('tis this it seems our Author would be at) 'as the fear of invisible powers, and the dismall apprehensions of the world to come: and for this very reason, though there were no other, it is fit they should be allowed the same honour and respect, as would be acknowledged their due, if they were sincere and honest men.' No Atheist could have said better.[1]   *R.T.* I, pp. 313–14.

Marvell also quotes 'from his first Book, p. 57' the remark:

'Some pert and pragmatical Divines, had filled the world with a Buzze and noise of the Divine Spirit;'

p. 323.

and from the Preface:

'Nonconformist Preachers do spend most of their Pulpit-sweat in making a noise about Communion with God.'[2]   p. 324.

And, for a final example:

The Nonconformist Preachers, you say, *make a grievous noise of the Lord* Christ, *talk loud of getting an interest in the Lord* Christ, *tell fine Romances of the secret Amours between the Believing Soul and the Lord* Christ, *and prodigious Stories of the miraculous feats of Faith in the Lord* Christ.[3] Did ever Divine rattle out such profane Balderdash! I cannot refrain, Sir, to tell you that you are not fit to have Christ in your mouth.[4]   *R.T.* II, p. 243.

Against Parker's extraordinary mixture of aggressiveness and levity Marvell for the most part fenced. But he does not trifle with the main question, and on occasion he drops all irony and states honestly and frankly those beliefs which underlie his mocking:

...yet because he questions me of my Belief (which I

[1] Grosart, *loc. cit.* pp. 219–20.   [2] *Ibid.* pp. 226–7.
[3] *Reproof*, p. 56.   [4] Grosart, *loc. cit.* pp. 420–1.

believe he never yet did to any man in his own Parsonages, or either at *Ickham* or *Chartham*) I do however count my self obliged to give him some answer, as much as he can challenge of me; that is, I do most certainly believe that the Supream Magistrate hath some Power, but not all Power in matters of Religion. pp. 93–4.

For Christianity has obliged Men to very hard Duty, and ransacks their very Thoughts, not being contented with an Unblameableness as to the Law, nor with an external Righteousness: It aims all at that which is sincere and solid, and having laid that weight upon the Conscience, which will be found sufficient for any honest Man to walk under, it hath not pressed and loaded Men further with the burthen of Ritual and Ceremonial Traditions and Impositions.[1] p. 205.

In pleading for every man's right to his own religious practices, if they involve no doctrinal heresies, Marvell relies upon the piety and good sense of the best of the Nonconformists, though he admits their occasional fanaticism. But in the age of the Conventicle and Five Mile Acts, fanaticism was no prerogative of the Nonconformists.[2] Parker was the less entitled to attack toleration in that till the Restoration converted him he had been a Presbyterian. At present, he exalted ceremonial above belief and allowed such absolute powers of determination in religion to the magistrate that, as Marvell pointed out, the people would be obliged to conform to Mohammedanism if it were imposed by law, or to commit mortal sin.

[1] Grosart, *loc. cit.* pp. 304, 391.
[2] Marvell once stood alone in the House to protest against the Conventicle Act. See *The Diary of John Milward, ed. cit.*, entry for 30 March 1668.

It is indeed obvious that to Parker Nonconformity is more intolerable for the standard of living
which it sets to the clergy than for any of its religious
tenets:

...you would wheedle them [the clergy] out of all the
comforts and advantages of life, and perswade them to
strip themselves of all the secular conveniencies wherewith
the wisdome and the bounty of former Ages have endowed
the Church.[1]

Marvell is not slow to apply the *argumentum ad
hominem* to such passages:

...I am so far from thinking enviously of the Revenue of
the Church of *England*, that...I think in my Conscience it is
all but too little, and wish with all my heart that there could
be some way found out to augment it. But in the mean
time, (to tell you my heart, for what needs dissembling
among friends?) I am inclinable to think, as the Revenue
now stands, there is sometimes an errour in the Distribu-
tion. And for example, I think it is a shame that such a one
as you should for writing of Political, flattering, persecuting,
scandalous Books, be recompens'd with more preferment,
then would comfortably maintain ten Godly Orthodox
and Conformable Ministers, who take care of the Peoples
Souls committed to their charge, and reside among them.
...You in the mean time, as if you were an Exempt of the
Clergy, and as Parson can transmit over the Cure of Souls
to your Curate, saunter about City and Countrey whither
your gilt Coach and extravagance will carry you, starving
your People, and pampring your Horses, so that a poor
man cannot approach their Heels without dying for't.[2]

pp. 133–35.

Marvell's theory of toleration is basically religious:
but it is related to a complete and coherent theory of

---

[1] *Reproof*, pp. 331–2.   [2] Grosart, *loc. cit.* pp. 335–7.

government which he states at length.[1] It is the duty
of the ruler to govern in such a way as shall ensure the
happiness of his subjects; this is his part of their mutual
obligation, whereby he himself, the ruler, is given
authority and revenue. In matters of religion it is an
abuse of his authority to enforce strict uniformity;
such an enforcement would, moreover, be inex-
pedient:

The Power of the Magistrate does most certainly issue
from the Divine Authority. The Obedience due to that
Power is by Divine Command; and Subjects are bound
both as Men and as Christians to obey the Magistrate
Actively in all things where their Duty to God intercedes
not, and however Passively, that is either by leaving their
Countrey, or if they cannot do that (the Magistrate or
the reason of their own occasions hindring them) then
by suffering patiently at home, without giving the least
publick disturbance....But the modester Question...
would be how far it is advisable for a Prince to exert and
push the rigour of that Power which no man can deny
him...The wealth of a Shepheard depends upon the
multitude of his flock, the good of their Pasture, and
the Quietness of their feeding: and Princes...cannot
expect any considerable increase to themselves, if by
continual terrour they amaze, shatter, and hare their
People, driving them into Woods, and running them upon
Precipices....There is not any Priviledge so dear, but it
may be extorted from Subjects by good usages, and by
keeping them always up in their good humour...it is
impossible but that even without reach or intention upon
the Princes part, all should fall into his hand, and in so
short a time the very memory or thoughts of any such
thing as Publick liberty would, as it were by consent,
expire and be forever extinguish'd.[2]   pp. 177–181.

---

[1] Grosart, *loc. cit.* pp. 368 ff.   [2] *Ibid.* pp. 370, 373.

The Puritan shows through the loyalist here. But in general Marvell trusts in the English capacity to evolve a suitable form of government as if by an instinctive process of self-adjustment. This is better if it is consciously and lawfully achieved; but if the rulers fail, the process will not delay:

> In all things that are insensible there is nevertheless a natural force always operating to expel and reject whatsoever is contrary to their subsistence....the common People in all places partake so much of Sense and Nature, that, could they be imagined and contrived to be irrational, yet they would ferment and tumultuate at last for their own preservation. Yet neither do they want the use of Reason, and perhaps their aggregated Judgment discerns most truly the Errours of Government, forasmuch as they are the first to be sure that smart under them. In this only they come to be short sighted; that though they know the Diseases, they understand not the Remedies; and though good Patients, they are ill Physicians. The Magistrate onely is authorized, qualified, and capable to make a just and effectual Reformation, and especially among the Ecclesiasticks.[1]   pp. 192–93.

It is in such passages, rather than in those where he is directly engaged with him, that Marvell most completely subdues the Archdeacon. They show not only the capacity to theorize but to observe: Marvell had seen during the events of 1659–60 how completely the common people could be good patients and ill physicians. Against the background of arbitrary government which prevailed in 1673 these are bold words, however, and probably dangerous ones; as addressed to one of the future tools of James II they have an irony now that they had not at the time.

[1] Grosart, *loc. cit.* p. 382.

On matters of government Marvell is much more sparing of wit than Parker, who had

> an Emulation of Wit, of which you ought to be a good Husband, for you come by it very hardly. Whether I have any at all I know not, neither further than it is not fit for me to reject any good quality wherewith God may have indued me, do I much care: but would be glad to part with it very easily for any thing intellectual, that is solid and useful.[1]   p. 231.

The literary virtue of *The Rehearsal Transpros'd* is then in the variety and vivacity of the methods which Marvell employed. Against a stiff and grandiose writer he used so many shades of irony, innuendo, ridicule, frontal attack, that his opponent could scarcely hope to reply effectively upon one level without exposing himself upon another. Marvell was provoked to turn Parker's own words directly against him, for though he attacked the 'lushious Metaphors' of the older school of divines[2] Parker was florid enough at times. Of a work which he suspected to be Parker's Marvell says:

> ...but as for his *brisk and laboured periods*, they may be traced every where. What say you to this for Example? *As the Profession of the Gospel is a most sacred thing, the Doctrine of the Gospel a most holy rule, the Author of our Religion an exemplar and patern of meekness: So when Christians renounce this Sacred Profession, lay aside this Holy Gospel, and abrenunciate Christ the pattern of meekness, they soon become the most desperate Villains in the World.* (*Bax. bap.* p. 1.) (Ay: very truly said were it but rightly applyed) Never in my life did I read any thing that more lively expresses and nicks the Energy of our Authors sense, or the ro-

---

[1] Grosart, *loc. cit.* p. 411.   [2] *Ecclesiastical Policy*, p. 76.

tundity and cadence of his Numbers...And therefore if perhaps he were not the Author, yet I dare undertake that when he came to the Licensing of that Pamphlet, he felt such an expansion of heart, such an adlubescence of mind, and such an exaltation of spirit, that betwixt Joy and Love he could scarce restrain from kissing it.[1]

pp. 101–102.

Marvell's criticism is often a literary criticism, and his moral objections take the form of a comment upon Parker's actual language. For instance, when Parker is urging that a subject ought to obey even against his conscience, because the responsibility is the State's and not his, Marvell observes:

...a man would suffer something rather than commit that little error against his Conscience, which must render him an Hypocrite to God, and a Knave amongst Men.... (And mark) *the Commands of Authority will warrant my Obedience, my Obedience will hallow, or at least excuse my action, and so secure me from sin if not from error*...Though the Subject made me serious, yet I could not reade the expression without laughter: *My Obedience will hallow, or at least excuse my Action.* So inconsiderable a difference he seems to make betwixt those terms, That if ever our Author come for his merits in election for to be a Bishop, a man might almost adventure instead of *Consecrated* to say that he was *Excused.*[2]

R.T. I, pp. 115, 116.

And later he flings the phrase in Bayes' teeth again: for he has a faculty for 'damnable iteration':

The Nonconformists have suffered as well as any men in the World, and could do so still if it were his Majesty's pleasure. Their *Duty to God hath hallowed*, and their *Duty to the Magistrate hath excused* both their Pain and Ignominy.[3]

pp. 129–130.

[1] Grosart, *loc. cit.* pp. 310–11.
[2] *Ibid.* pp. 84–85.   [3] *Ibid.* p. 94.

He takes any opportunity to deflate Parker or use his lapses of language against him, perhaps with the more pleasure because Parker belonged to the new reforming school of pulpit eloquence. In *A Free and Impartial Censure of the Platonick Philosophy* (1666) he had bitterly attacked the older divines, and in particular Jeremy Taylor, whose style excited his mirth incontinently. With his friend Simon Patrick, Parker had even shared in Seth Ward's scheme for a universal language of a mathematical kind. But for the involutions of the periodic style he substituted a flatly hectoring manner. His style is perfect Bayes. In *The Reproof* he thus addresses Marvell:

You have indeed taken the Advantage (though it is cowardly and dishonourably done to take it) of accosting me in such a clownish and licentious way of writing, as you know to be unsuitable both to the Civility of my Education, and the Gravity of my Profession....And by that time I have dispatcht all that I shall think convenient to chastise the folly and rashness of your Undertaking, I am pretty confident you will have so much reason to look simply, that the company will be fully satisfied there will be but little need of sending for a witty man to put you out of countenance.[1]

It is bludgeon against rapier. Marvell's grand manner is of another kind; is, as the Archdeacon observes, that 'of a well-bred and fashionable Gentleman'.[2] It was this which made it so unlikely and so timely an aid to the Nonconformist cause. Having caught Parker citing John Hales as if he had read him, and at the same time attributing to Marvell words which

---

[1] *Reproof*, pp. 1-2.   [2] *Ibid.* p. 274.

were actually a quotation from Hales, Marvell with a courtly flourish declines the argument:

> I yeild Mr. *Bayes*, and instead of admiring *that Majesty and Beauty which sits upon the Forehead of Masculine Truth and generous Honesty*, I will henceforward admire only the *maidenly modesty*, & *rosial blushes* that bloom on *your* Cheeks and inhabit *your* Forehead.[1]
>
> *R.T.* II, p. 307.

This is the technique of Marvell's satiric conversation with the priest in *Fleckno*: and it is exquisitely adapted to the weakness of Bayes. At other times Marvell will use the most familiar and colloquial language for direct attack:

> ...you were so hungry at that time, that you would have ador'd an Onion, so it had cryed, *Come eat me*.[2]   p. 241.

> ...he hastened to bring himself in plight by such common remedies as were next to hand, writing too all the while by girds and snatches hand over head.[3]   p. 19.

> ...your Book being full and crawling all over with such expressions.[4]   p. 256.

The concreteness of the writing, with the play of metaphors in nouns and verbs, the reference to items of news, proverbs, current jests, is not merely contrasted with the pomposity of Bayes: Marvell often rounds off his own more serious arguments with some sudden thrust of familiar contempt. In the following passage, for example, the long first sentence unfolds a case, upon which judgment is pronounced with brief emphasis. In each sentence the mode of attack

---

[1] Grosart, *loc. cit.* p. 471.   [2] *Ibid.* p. 419.
[3] *Ibid.* p. 246.   [4] *Ibid.* p. 432.

changes: it is direct in the first, by innuendo in the second and by sarcasm in the third:

> But you imagine doubtless, and do not a little applaud yourself for the Invention; that by the Doctrine of punishing Non-conformity more severely than the foulest Immorality, you have made your self the Head of a Party, and a World of People will clutter henceforward to shelter themselves under the Wing of your Patronage. I confess it is a great and brave undertaking, and which, I believe, none ever managed before, nor will be so hardy as to take it up again for the future: Let it be Ingraven on your Tomb.[1]   p. 265.

At other times, by taking the metaphors in a literal sense, and by reading in a general way what was meant as a particular instance, by the sudden evoking of incongruous fancies, or the drawing of logical but improbable conclusions, Marvell subverts the argument. This purely verbal fencing was also practised by his opponents, but it really belongs to an earlier age: for instance in his long playing with the unfortunate title page of Bayes' book, Marvell recalls the similar passages in Milton's *Apology...for Smectymnuus* (a tract which is several times quoted by both sides). Such methods now appear sophistical and tedious, though Marvell, thanks to his sense of humour, usually makes the points lightly enough.

There were of course personal issues involved, particularly Parker's attack on Milton, whose friend he had been in earlier days: Marvell's warm defence is well known. Hales, too, who was by this time dead, he clears from several charges. In the Second Part,

---

[1] Grosart, *loc. cit.* p. 438.

where Marvell became on the whole distinctly more personal, he was replying to the very scurrilous attacks of the anonymous pamphleteers, as well as to the letter 'left at a friend's house' and concluding 'If thou darest to Print or Publish another Lie or Libel upon Doctor Parker, By the Eternal God I will cut thy Throat'. His printer had been pilloried. To which Marvell retorted by publishing the Second Part under his own name, and he tells Parker how little he heeds

> your threatning me here and in several other places with the loss of mine Ears, which however are yet in good plight, and apprehend no other danger, Mr. *Bayes* but to be of your Auditory.[1]   p. 114.

To write at all, as Marvell explains, seems to him a dangerous employment, though not for Bayes' reason: it is more dangerous to write satire, and especially dangerous to undertake correction of the clergy. Yet this may be a public duty if it is undertaken for the defence of principles and the correction of manners. He sets out his apology at some length:

> . . . neither could I ever discover before such an exuberance in mine own, either abilities, which I am sensible how mean, or yet in my inclination, that should tempt me from that modest retiredness to which I had all my life time hitherto been addicted.[2]   p. 45.

The Rehearsal Transpros'd is therefore far from being a mere burlesque, as Burnet implies; it does not all consist of walking 'in the Garden' and gathering 'some of Mr *Bayes* his Flowers'.

---

[1] Grosart, *loc. cit.* p. 320.   [2] *Ibid.* p. 267.

Marvell's tolerance and his just sense of what was important endorsed his irony. He was disinterested in the controversy: for he was himself a churchman and the son of a churchman: he held no brief for sectaries. But toleration seemed to him a first principle of ecclesiastical as well as of temporal government: and too close an alliance between ecclesiastical and temporal government was in his view more dangerous for the Church than for the State.

Apart from its intrinsic interest, *The Rehearsal Transpros'd* deserves recognition for its place in literary history. In the flexibility of his attack, Marvell produced what might roughly be taken as the prose version of the 'metaphysical' style. There is the same synchronization of the important with the trivial, the same free combination of colloquialism and learning, the same variety in the points of view. He cites at some length 'that witty fable of Doctor Donne' *The Progress of the Soul*, gives a résumé, and applies it to Parker. He parodies the style of Dryden's dedications, and refers with appreciation to *Hudibras*. His familiar quoting of Chaucer[1] shows a more surprising catholicity.

The style, though always plain, easy and fluent, is a little too familiar to have gained the approval of the new purists. He will say 'you had by this breath only cool'd your own Porridge', or even 'This Story would have been Nuts to Mother Midnight'. Parker, in attempting to deal with Marvell's charge that he kept a mistress, says:

... as for your rude and uncivil language, I am willing to

---

[1] Grosart, *loc. cit.* p. 364.

impute it to your first unhappy Education among Boat-
Swains and Cabin-Boys,[1] whose Phrases as you learn'd
in your Childhood, so it is not to be expected you should
ever unlearn them by your Conversation with the Bear-
herds of *Barn*, the Canibals of *Geneva*.[2]

There are actually no Provincialisms and certainly
no Billingsgate in Marvell (if he inclines in any way
it is to Gallicism): but he did not exclude the kind of
phrases that Swift would have put into his *Genteel and
Ingenious Conversation*. His standards were not those of
'rotundity and cadence of...Numbers' of the Archdeacon: and for pamphlet skirmishings his own had
the advantage, for it has been shown with what ease
he could control and vary the rhythm and length of
his sentences, or drop from a grand manner, with its
appropriate vocabulary, to a very familiar mode of
speech. A consequence of this flexibility is his readiness
to assume the voice of his opponent, to write burlesque.
When the Archdeacon had written a pretended proclamation in the king's name,[3] Marvell capped it by
writing one 'for the toleration of debauchery' in the
name of his enemy: 'By the Archdeacon...Bayes
R....' The power of Marvell to detect latent and
unintentional meanings in the words of Parker is a
necessary appendix to his own very complete and
conscious control:

Gods Moral accomplishments! If it were an Oath,
I should not think it binds me: But in the mean time
methinks it has something in it bordering upon Blasphemy.[4]

p. 242.

[1] Perhaps this was because Marvell had called Parker 'a person of
considerable ecclesiastical tunnage'.

[2] *Reproof*, p. 227.   [3] *Ibid.* p. 64.   [4] Grosart, *loc. cit.* p. 420.

While the Archdeacon theorizes about standards
of correctness, Marvell remains conversational, and
the tone of his conversation varies from the familiar
to the superciliously elegant. One of his modern
habits is the use of the disdainful *really*: 'but really
I consult mine ease', 'I must walk faster for really I
take cold'.

In the long passage beginning 'Those that take
upon themselves to be Writers'[1] Marvell gives some of
his own views. He considers it dangerous for the
writer to assume that he can either entertain or im-
prove others: and it is still more dangerous for him
to write from motives of personal ambition:

> For indeed whosoever he be that comes in Print, where-
> as he might have sate at home in quiet, does either make a
> Treat, or send a Challenge to all Readers; in which cases,
> the first, it concerns him to have no scarcity of Provisions,
> and in the other to be compleatly Arm'd: for if any thing
> be amiss on either part, Men are subject to scorn the
> weakness of the Attaque, or laugh at the meanness of
> the Entertainment.   pp. 24–5.

This modesty ('So that not to Write at all is much the
safer course of life') may perhaps explain why Marvell
published only strictly utilitarian or public work;
poems on great men and national occasions, or com-
ments on governmental affairs. Several characteristics
of Marvell's style—the constant shift of the angle of
attack, the parody, and the preoccupation with
verbal minutiae—suggest a connection with the
greatest satirist of the next age. This is particularly

[1] Grosart, *loc. cit.* pp. 250 ff.

seen in Swift's first work, *A Tale of a Tub*, written twenty-three years after *The Rehearsal Transpros'd*.[1]

Swift's indebtedness to Marvell has been noted by M. Legouis[2] and by Professor Nichol Smith.[3] They have been concerned chiefly with detailed borrowings; the story of throwing out a tub to divert a whale,[4] the theory that a straight line produced to infinity becomes a circle[5] and other verbal correspondences.[6]

The actual subject of the *Tale*, the relation of ceremonies to doctrine, is of course the same as the subject of Marvell's pamphlet, and in the Author's Apology[7] Swift acknowledges the power of *The Rehearsal Transpros'd*. In some passages Marvell compares favourably with Swift: for example the miraculous feats of Peter in Section IV are hardly equal to the medicinal account of *The Rehearsal Transpros'd*:

Now, this *Pickle*, to the Taste, the Smell, and the Sight, appeared exactly the same, with what is in common Service for Beef, and Butter, and Herrings, (and has been

[1] It may be worth noting that Swift's friend Robert Harley, Earl of Oxford, was the son of Sir Edward Harley, Marvell's friend, to whom he wrote freely about his prose. (*V*. Chapter VI.)

[2] *André Marvell*, pp. 385, 431.

[3] *A Tale of a Tub*, ed. Guthkelch and Nichol Smith, p. lvi.

[4] *A Tale of a Tub*, ed. cit. p. 40; Grosart, *loc. cit.* p. 313.

[5] *A Tale of a Tub*, ed. cit. p. 158; Grosart, *loc. cit.* pp. 146, 314.

[6] There are a few more, such as the comparison of the pulpit with the stage and the gallows (*A Tale of a Tub*, ed. cit. pp. 58 ff.; Grosart, *loc. cit.* pp. 262 ff.), the fanatic on predestination (*A Tale of a Tub*, ed. cit. pp. 192–3; Grosart, *loc. cit.* p. 235), the madness of Peter (*A Tale of a Tub*, ed. cit. pp. 114 ff.), and the madness of Bayes (Grosart, *loc. cit.* pp. 50–1), and two other passages which seem to suggest the chapter of the Aeolists (Grosart, *loc. cit.* pp. 426, 454).

[7] *A Tale of a Tub*, ed. cit. p. 10.

often applied that way with great Success) but for its many Sovereign Virtues was a quite different Thing. For *Peter* would put in a certain Quantity of his *Powder Pimperlim pimp*, after which it never failed of Success. The Operation was performed by *Spargefaction* in a proper Time of the Moon. The Patient who was to be *pickled*, if it were a House, would infallibly be preserved from all Spiders, Rats, and Weazels; If the Party affected were a Dog, he should be exempt from Mange, and Madness, and Hunger. It also infallibly took away all Scabs and Lice, and scall'd Heads from Children, never hindring the Patient from any Duty, either at Bed or Board.[1]

But whatever old mischief may possibly lurk in his Body; I am told by one, who pretends to the best intelligence, That this was a new Disease....To be short, as I am certainly inform'd, he was sick of *the Rehearsal Transpros'd*....I am sorry if that should occasion a distemper, which [I] ordered as Physick; the *Rehearsal Transpros'd* being too only a particular prescription in his case, and not to be applyed to others without special direction. But some curious persons would be licking at it, and most Men finding it not distastful to the Palate, it grew in a short time to be of common use in the Shops. I perceive that it wrought a sensible alteration in all that took it; but varying in some for the better, in others for the worse, according to the difference of their Complexions. Some were swoln up to the Throat, some their Heads turn'd round, and others it made their Hearts ake; but all these were but a few in number; most Men found only a little tingling in their Ears, and after its greatest violence, it discharged it self in an innocent fit of uncessant laughter.[2]   pp. 16–17.

Such a passage has more in common with the chapter on the Academy of Projectors in the third book of *Gulliver's Travels*, the earliest to be written.

[1] *A Tale of a Tub*, ed. cit. pp. 109–10.
[2] Grosart, *loc. cit.* pp. 244–5.

In *A Tale of a Tub* Swift generally works with larger units than the single paragraph; his style in this work appears exuberant, simple and cumulative in its effect; but of course does not represent him at his best. The finest and most characteristic writing is in the digressions, and if the famous passage on the dissection of a beau[1] be compared with the passage on the dissection of Parker, the advantage is with Swift:

> And yet withall that it hath been thus far the odiousest task that ever I undertook, and has look'd to me all the while like the cruelty of a Living Dissection, which, however it may tend to publick instruction, and though I have pick'd out the most noxious Creature to be anatomiz'd, yet doth scarse excuse or recompence the offensiveness of the scent and fouling of my fingers.[2]   p. 78.

Marvell is unimplicated, in a position of unassailable superiority, like the Emperor of Brobdingnag examining the little odious vermin of Gulliver's race, and therefore he can conclude:

> But if I have undergone the drudgery of the more loathsom part already, I will not defraud my self of what is more truly pleasant, and remains behind the lighter burthen, the conflict with, if it may be so call'd his Reason.   pp. 78–9.

That suspended qualification gives by implication Marvell's detached and unexerted power. He is really enjoying himself, in the manner in which Swift enjoyed himself only in the *Bickerstaff Papers*. If the issue is a serious one, it is not consistently serious for Marvell in the personal way in which Swift's writing

---

[1] *A Tale of a Tub*, ed. cit. pp. 173–4.
[2] Grosart, *loc. cit.* p. 292.

is serious. The self-questioning, the probing and the
negative conclusions which lie behind the shifts and
transitions from level to level in the satire of Swift
are not paralleled in Marvell. The loathing of the
bestiality of human beings which comes out in Swift's
metaphors from animals is poles apart from Marvell's
description of the hunting of the magpie, or his observation of Parker's malice towards bystanders in
the quarrel:

> Hence also, and upon the same natural ground, it is
> the wisdome of Cats to whet their Claws against the Chairs
> and Hangings, in meditation of the next *Rat* they are to
> encounter.[1]   *R.T.* i, p. 81.

—or the fatness of Parker, suddenly mentioned along
with his jealousy:

> The great little Animal was on a sudden turn'd so
> Yellow, and grown withall so unwieldy, that he might
> have past currant for the Elephant upon a Guinny.[2]
>   *R.T.* ii, p. 18.

Swift can only do this in his *jeux d'esprit*, where his
delight in his own nimbleness is exercising itself upon
some subject trivial throughout, and he is triumphing
over Mr Partridge or other ostensible opponents:

> Without entering into Criticism of *Chronology* about the
> Hour of his Death; I shall only prove, that Mr *Partrige* is not
> alive. And my first Argument is thus: Above a Thousand
> Gentlemen having bought his Almanacks for this Year,
> meerly to find what he said against me; at every Line they
> read, they would lift up their Eyes, and cry out, betwixt
> Rage and Laughter, *They were sure no Man* alive *ever writ
> such damned Stuff as this*.[3]

---

[1] Grosart, *loc. cit.* p. 60.   [2] *Ibid.* p. 246.

[3] *A Vindication of Isaac Bickerstaff, Esq.*; *Prose Works*, ed. Herbert
Davies (Shakespeare Head Press, 1939), Vol. ii, p. 162.

This is exactly the kind of ridicule Marvell used against Parker; but Swift would never have employed it where his principles or his feelings were deeply engaged. Marvell can afford to do so, because he has a security of unquestioned and untroubled belief which gives him a standard by which he can relate the different levels of feeling, with their intensity. The power of Swift as a writer depending as it does on destruction and negation, whilst it compels variety, allows of no contrast in any strict sense of that word. The distinction between the liberty which their beliefs accord to Swift and Marvell is that between parole and freedom. Even in *A Tale of a Tub*, which, as Dr Johnson says, 'exhibits a vehemence and rapidity of mind, a copiousness of images, and vivacity of diction, such as he afterwards never possessed, or never exerted',[1] the peculiar exhilaration derives from the successive series of arguments abandoned;[2] and the pressure of negation which dictates their rejection is constant.

Marvell on the other hand both shifts his ground and relaxes at times: it does not make him a greater writer that he could deal with one subject both in the mood of the *Bickerstaff Papers* and of *A Tale of a Tub*: for this is a matter of range, and not of penetration. It was possible because Marvell could, if necessary, as Swift never could, take up a simple straightforward affirmative, and state it serenely:

...yet because he questions me of my Belief...I do how-

---

[1] Johnson, *Life of Swift*.
[2] This last point is F. R. Leavis's, *Determinations* (Chatto and Windus, 1934).

ever count my self obliged to give him some answer, as much as he can challenge of me; that is, I do most certainly believe that the Supream Magistrate hath some Power, but not all Power, in matters of Religion.[1]

R.T. II, pp. 93–4.

That kind of security Swift never had, either in his private or his public writing: and though he could, without it, write great prose, the lack cut him off from poetry.

[1] It is tempting to simplify by saying that Marvell believed the Beatitudes to be a surer guide to salvation than the Thirty Nine Articles. But he recognizes, of course, the State's function in religion and the Magistrate's duty and power in religious matters. The problem is a problem of adjustment. The issue had been put succinctly in *A Holy Commonwealth,... Written by Richard Baxter at the invitation of James Harrington Esquire...*, *1659*, p. 285:

'*Thes. 246. The Civil Power is Essential to a Commonwealth (or Civil Polity) and the Pastors only necessary to its well-being, and the Pastors are essential to the Church (as a Political Society) and the Magistrate necessary but to its well-being.*

A Church may possibly be without a Magistrate, but not well: And a Common-wealth may possibly be without the Pastors of the Church or other Ministers of Christ; but not well.'

For an account of the problem, see W. K. Jordan, *The Development of Religious Toleration in England* (Allen and Unwin, 3 vols., 1932–7): this includes biographies of Baxter, Hales, Owen and others.

V

MINOR PAMPHLETS AND LETTERS

The Rehearsal Transpros'd was in an important social trend; it is an attempt to solve by means of toleration the religious problems of the century. It adds to the scholarly pleas of the 'Latitude men' and Marvell's own friends, such as Hales and Owen, an appeal which could reach the ordinary laic and even the irreligious wit, though his phrase 'I think the Cause too good to have been fought for' struck most of his opponents as perfectly absurd and they do not tire of twitting him about the 'Cause Too Good, or the Good Old Cause'.

His other pamphlets are more finished, less lively, and they cut less deep. There are perhaps finer passages in *Mr Smirke*, but it is a less serious work. Having spoken out once, Marvell did not do so again.

The subject and occasion were similar to those which produced *The Rehearsal Transpros'd*, but Marvell was not now coming to the rescue of friends like Milton, but only of Herbert Croft, Bishop of Hereford, to whose letters of thanks he replied with an overwhelming politeness.[1] And his opponent Francis Turner was by no means such an astonishing figure as Samuel Parker; at this time Master of St John's College, Cambridge, and Chaplain to the Duke of York, he was later to win fame as one of the Seven Bishops; and he seems

[1] Both letters were sent by Marvell to Will Popple. See p. 134.

both less formidable and less worldly than the other, for he remained faithful to James and died a non-juror.

The controversy arose out of a pamphlet, which the Bishop had originally meant to present to Parliament, but, as the House was prorogued, it became public. It was entitled *The Naked Truth*,[1] and argued for toleration from the state of the primitive Church. Turner wrote his *Animadversions* in reply; and as both it and *The Naked Truth* were anonymous, he had contrived to be very rude to his superior. In *Mr Smirke*[2] Marvell stepped in: the title was taken from a character in Etherege's play *The Man of Mode*.

The first point is Mr Smirke's defect in learning, charity, and sense:

> So that being the man pitched upon, he took up an unfortunate resolution that he would be Witty. Infortunate I say, and no less Criminal: for I dare aver that never any person was more manifestly guilty of the sin against Nature.[3]　　　　　　　　　　　　p. 4.

> [Mr Smirke] tells him pleasantly that, *Hell it self is full of such as were once full of Good Intentions*: 'tis a Concluding piece of Wit, and therefore, as well as for the Rarity, should be civilly treated and incouraged;...if this be the qualification of such as go to Hell, the Animadverter hath secured himself from coming there and so many more as were his Partners.[4]　　　　　　　p. 14.

Marvell defends the Bishop for printing without

[1] Edited by Herbert Hensley Henson, then Bishop of Hereford (Chatto and Windus, 1919).

[2] *Mr. Smirke; or, the Divine in Mode: being Certain Annotations, upon the Animadversions on the Naked Truth. Together with a Short Historical Essay, concerning General Councils, Creeds, and Impositions, in Matters of Religion...By Andreas Rivetus, Junior, Anagr. Res Nuda Veritas. Printed Anno Domini MDCLXXVI.*

[3] Grosart, *Works*, vol. IV, p. 11.　　　　[4] *Ibid.* pp. 27–8.

I

a licence. Croft had not authorized the publication
of the pamphlet: he had had it printed for Members
of Parliament only. Marvell even justifies the book-
seller who put it into general circulation:

> ...considering how empty of late the Church Magazines
> have been of that Spiritual Armour, which the Apostle
> found sufficient against the assaults of whatsoever enemy,
> even of Satan; what could men, in all humane reason do
> less, then to furnish such of the Clergy as wanted, with
> these Weapons of another Warfare?[1]   p. 8.

He invents a theory that the author of *The Naked
Truth* has bewitched the Animadverter:

> And indeed the Animadverter hath many times in the
> day such Fits take him, wherein he is lifted up in the Aire
> that six men cannot hold him down, teares, raves, and
> foams at the mouth, casts up all kind of trash, somtimes
> speakes *Greek* and *Latine*, that no man but would swear he
> is bewitched: and this never happens but when the Author
> appeares to him.[2]   p. 17.

He is obliged to deal with Mr Smirke at such length
only because of the scurrilities which he has written,
for

> Calumny is like *London*-dirt, with which though a man
> may be spatter'd in an instant, yet it requires much time,
> pains, and Fullers-earth to scoure it out again.[3]   p. 14.

The more serious part reiterates the views of
Marvell's earlier work: he considers the Apostles'
Creed sufficient in the way of declaration of faith to
secure a man from persecution,[4] which in any case
should not be used:

St. *Paul* hath said, *God forbid we should do evil that good*

---

[1] Grosart, *loc. cit.* p. 18.   [2] *Ibid.* p. 32.
[3] *Ibid.* p. 28.   [4] *Ibid.* p. 40.

*may come of it.....*No man ought to cheat another
though to the true beliefe: Not by Interlining the Scripture. Not by false Quotation of Scripture, or of a Father.
Not by forging a Heathen Prophecy, or altering an
Author. Not by a false Syllogisme: Not by telling a lye
for God.... [1]   p. 40.

He concludes "this reasonable transport" with
remarking that there is no Scriptural warrant for
force.

Marvell's capacity to quote Scripture is very well
illustrated in these pages. He must have known his
New Testament pretty well by heart. He caps
the Bishop's citations: 'May I add one, Marke 9.
17'.[2] And he ends with an anecdote which turns
on the instant recognition of a text, concerning a
certain Vice-Chancellor who forcibly haled some
Nonconformists to St Mary's to hear a sermon,
saying 'Compel them to come in'. But unfortunately
for the Vice-Chancellor the texts were Acts v. 41 and
Matt. x. 16.

After an attempt to go through Mr Smirke's
pamphlet, Marvell finds it too tedious to be borne:
he gives it up and writes instead an *Essay on General
Councils*. This is of course directed against the authority
and jurisdiction of the Bishops, and Marvell argues
learnedly on the futility of the Councils of the Early
Church. Later he said that people confessed it 'was
writ well to the purpose, but that it was a very ill
purpose'. At all events he silenced Mr Smirke, but
according to himself that was not much of an exploit:

He is a meer Kitchin-Plunderer, and attacks but the

[1] Grosart, *loc. cit.* pp. 73, 82.   [2] *Ibid.* p. 42.

Baggage, where even the Suttlers would be too hard for
him.[1]   93ᵛ.

The *Essay on General Councils* is interesting as showing
Marvell's developing power to write in the logical
style of modern controversy. M. Legouis gratefully
records that this, alone of the earlier works, can be
summarized. Its virtues are paid for, however, by
the loss of that vivid, sprightly, colloquial vocabulary
which is the medium of the other part of the pamphlet.
Marvell had been tamed. Literary interests must remain more grateful for *Mr Smirke*, where the ease
and comprehensiveness of the satire extends from
Mr Smirke to controversial divines in general. Its
opening is among Marvell's finest pieces of satiric
writing and must be quoted in full:

It hath been the Good Nature (and Politicians will
have it the Wisdom) of most Governours to entertain the
people with Publick Recreations; and therefore to in-
courage such as could best contribute to their Divertisement. And hence doubtless it is, that our Ecclesiastical
Governours also (who as they yield to none for Prudence,
so in good Humor they exceed all others,) have not dis-
dained of late years to afford the Laity no inconsiderable
Pastime. Yea so great hath been their condescension that,
rather then faile, they have carried on the Merriment by
men of their own Faculty, who might otherwise by the
gravity of their Calling, have claimed an exemption from
such Offices....Yet, though the Clergy have hereby
manifested that nothing comes amiss to them, and
particularly, that when they give their minds to it, no
sort of men are more proper or capable to make sport
for Spectators; it hath so happened by the rewards and
Promotions bestowed upon those who have labour'd in

[1] Grosart, *loc. cit.* p. 83.

this Province, that many others in hopes of the like Preferment, although otherwise by their Parts, their Complexion and Education unfitted for this Jocular Divinity,
have in order to it wholly neglected the more weighty
cares of their Function. And from hence it proceeds,
that to the no small scandal and disreputation of our
Church, a great *Arcanum* of their State hath been dis-
covered and divulged: That, albeit Wit be not incon-
sistent and incompatible with a Clergy-man, yet neither
is it inseparable from them.... pp. 1–2.

Before men be admitted to so important an employment, it were fit they underwent a severe Examination;
and that it might appear, first, whether they have any
Sense: for without that how can any man pretend, and
yet they do, to be ingenious? Then, whether they have
any Modesty: for without that they can only be scurrilous and impudent. Next, whether any Truth: for true
Jests are those that do the greatest execution. And
Lastly, it were not amiss that they gave some account too
of their Christianity: for the world has always hitherto
been so uncivil as to expect somthing of that from the
Clergy; in the design and stile even of their lightest and
most uncanonical Writings.[1] p. 3.

Here the resemblance to Swift comes out with
particular clearness. The innocent asides ('how can
any man pretend, and yet they do, to be ingenious?'),
the weighting of a blow by invoking deliberately
inadequate public standards ('the world has always
hitherto been so uncivil...'), the pretended absorption
in manifest trivialities, the hard spare vocabulary,
might all be Swift's.

The pamphlet achieved its object, and went into
a second impression: while the *Essay on General
Councils* had been reprinted four times by 1703,

[1] Grosart, *loc. cit.* pp. 6–7.

either separately or in collections. No one attempted to reply, and the Bishop of Hereford might consider himself vindicated.

Marvell's next prose work was of a more unconventional and daring nature. This is the celebrated *Mock Speech from the Throne* (*His Majesty's Most Gracious Speech to Both Houses of Parliament*). The date of this in the best manuscript copy is 13 April 1675. Although both the date and the attribution have been questioned, it is impossible not to agree with M. Legouis that the evidence of the style is as strong as it could be. The external evidence also, such as it is, points to Marvell. It was perhaps the riskiest thing he ever did and it carries on the tradition of the mock-battle in *The last Instructions to a Painter* but applies the method even more maliciously. As a *grande geste* and a brilliant burlesque the speech deserves to be quoted in full. The accent of a living voice is caught, and also the air of ingenuous logic which Charles could so perfectly assume:[1]

[1] There are several earlier mock speeches in Marvell's writings, e.g. the Proclamation of Bayes. Hickeringill in his *Gregory Father Greybeard* composed several for Marvell. In the MS. from which the above version is printed (B.M. Add. 34,362) there is another, 'The Kings Speech from Oxford', dated 1680. This one exists in four MS. versions, and an early printed version in the British Museum entitled *Horse and A-Way* or a *S- before Parting* by Parson Hickeringil. The date is given as 1669, but though most of the references which might date it are left out of the speech, the ones to the Bankers (i.e. the Stop of the Exchequer, 1672) and to Mistress Hide and Emerton (appearing as 'Mr Hyde and Mrs Sutton') show that it bears a false date and that the version given is only a shortened and not an early draft. Since Hickeringill's name is attached, Marvell may have been responsible. The name of the printer is 'C. Banckes', i.e. Christopher Barker, the King's Printer! Moreover the sense is so garbled, and the

The K's Speech April 13th '75

My Lords and Gentlemen, I told you last Meeting, the Winter was the only time for business, and truly I thought so till my Ld Treasurer assur'd me that the Spring is the fittest season for Sallads and Subsidyes. I hope therfore this April will not prove so unnatural as not to afford plenty of both. Some of you may perhaps think it dangerous to make me too rich, but doe not fear it, for I promise you faithfully, whatsoever You will give I will always take care to want; for the truth of which you may rely upon the word of a King.

My Lords and Gentlemen, I can bear my owne straits with Patience, but my Ld-Treasurer protests that the Revenue, as it now stands, is too little for us both; one of us must pinch for it, if you do not help us out. I must speak freely to You I am under Incumbrances, for besides my Harlots in service my Reformado ones lye hard upon me. I have a pretty good Estate I confess, but Godsfish I have a great Charge upon it. Here is my Ld Treas^r can tell you that all the Mony designed for the Summer Guards must of necessity be employ'd to the next Yeares Cradles and Swadling-Cloths. What then shall we do for ships? I only hint this to You, it is Your Business, not mine. I know by Experience I can live without them, I lived ten Yeares without them abroad and was never in better health in my Life. But how will you live without them you had best say; and there-

poem which fills the other half of the sheet, *Vox and Lachrymae Anglorum*, is cut with such disregard for its sense that the text is only a curiosity. MS. Add. 34,362 is the most accurate text as regards proper names and annotations. It alone gives the date, the references to Lord St John and Lord Vaughan, and the correct names 'Mistress Hide and Emerton'. This affair is mentioned by Marvell in the *Letters to Hull*, Nos. 174, 176, *Miscellaneous Letters*, No. 21, and also in two poems, *The Statue in Stocks-Market* and *A Dialogue between the Two Horses....* The story is given in the notes to Margoliouth's edition: it was the *cause célèbre* of the spring of 1675, and Marvell was evidently particularly shocked by this attempt to force bigamy on a young girl.

fore I do not intend to insist upon it. There is another which I must press more ernestly, which is, it seemes a good part of my Revenue will faile in two or three Yeares, except You will be pleas'd to continue it. Now I have this to say for it, Pray why did you give me as much except you resolv'd to go on? The Nation hates you already, for giving so much, and I will hate you now if you doe not give me more. So that now your Interest obliges You to stick to me or you will not have a friend left in England. On the other side, if you will continue the Revenue as desired, I shall be inabled to performe those Great things for Your Religion and Libertye which I have had long in my Thoughts, but cannot effect them without this Establishment. Therefore look to it, if You do not make me Rich enough to undoe You, it shall lye at your dores; for my part I can with a cleare Conscience say, I have done my best and I shall leave the rest to my Sucessor. That I may gain Your good Opinion, the best way is to acquaint You with what I have done to deserve it, out of my Royall care for your *Religion* and your *Property*.

For the first, my late *Proclamation*[1] is a true Picture of my Mind: he that cant as in a Glass see my Zeal for the Church of England, doth not deserve any further satisfaction, for I declare him Wilfull, Abominable and not Good. Some may perhaps be startled and crye— how comes this sudden Change? To which I answer, I am a Changeling, I think that is a full Answre. But to convince Men that I mean as I say there are three Arguments. First, I tell You so, and you know I never broke my word. Secondly my Lord Treasurer says so, and he never told a Lye. Thirdly, my Lord Lauderdale will undertake for me, and I should be loath by any Act of mine to forfeit the Credit he hath with you.

If You desire more instances of my Zeal, I have them for You. For Example, I have converted all my Natural Sons from Popery and may say without Vanity, it was my owne Worke, and so much the more peculiar than the

[1] In the margin, *For Indulgance.*

begetting of them. It would do Your Heart good to hear how prettily little George can read in the Psalter.

They are all fine Children, God bless 'em, and so like me in their Understandings. But as I was saying I have to please you given a Pention to your favourite, the Lord Lauderdale, not so much that I thought he wanted it, as I thought You would take it kindly. I have made Portsmouth a Dutches, and have marryed her sister to my Lord of Pembroke. I have att my Brother's request sent my Lord of Inchequin to settle Protestant Religion at Tangier and my Ld Vaughan to propagate Christian Religion at Jamaica. I have made the Reverend and Learned Crew Bishop of Durham and att the first word of my Lady Portsmouth, I have preferr'd Bridock to be Bishop of Chichester. Now for your Propertyes, my behaviour to the Banckers and letting the Customes to my Ld St John and his partners take for publick Instances, and my proceeding between Mistress Hide and Emerton for a private one, as such convincing Evidences, that it will be needless to say more. I must now acquaint you, that by my Ld Treas^{r}s advice I have made a considerable Retrenchment upon my Expences of Candles and Charcoal, and do not intend to stop there but will, with your helpe looke into the late Embesselments of my Kitchinstuffe, for which by the way on my Conscience [neither] the Lord Treasurer nor my Lord Lauderdale are Guilty. I speake my Opinion, but if you shall find them daubing in that business I tell you plainly I leave them to you, for I would have the World know, I am not a Man to be cheated.

My Lords and Gentlemen, I desire you to believe of me as You have ever found, and I doe solemnly promise that whatsoever you give me shall be manag'd with the same Conduct, Thrift and Prudence, that I have ever practis'd since my happy Restauration.

For its full appreciation, this requires a study of the sedate account of the actual speech itself, as despatched by Marvell to the burgesses of Hull.[1] The fact that the Commons were petitioning for the removal of Lauderdale, and trying to impeach Danby the Treasurer, that the incredible public corruption had gone so far that even a House of which a third were in the King's pay had begun to jib at it, did not prevent Marvell from assuring his constituents that there were speeches of thanks on all sides; and he adds:

The Lords ordered that the Kings and the Lord Keepers Speeches should be printed which we expect will be out to morrow morning.[2]

It seems improbable, however, that Marvell could at this time actually have written his Mock Speech unless he had tossed it off overnight, for the closeness of the parody (especially in the opening paragraphs relating to the Navy) is such that he must have composed it after Charles' speech had really been delivered.[3]

Marvell was becoming more and more absorbed in the political situation, and his only return to religious topics, *Remarks upon a Late Disingenuous Discourse*, has not his usual interest. It defended John Howe, but argued on a subject which Marvell shrank from publicly discussing, the question of predestination. He therefore resorted merely to quipping his opponent and that without much flow of spirits. One suspects that the work was undertaken out of personal regard for Howe, formerly one of Cromwell's chaplains, but so tolerant and gentle that he was protected

[1] Margoliouth, *Letters to Hull*, No. 169.
[2] *Ibid*. No. 170.
[3] A shortened version of Charles' own speech may be found in Arthur Bryant's *Letters and Speeches of Charles II* (Cassell and Co. 1932).

after the Restoration by those whom he had protected
earlier. He lived to play a part in the events of 1688,
and to exercise charity and sympathy in those difficult
times.

Marvell's other work, *An Account of the Growth of
Popery, and Arbitrary Government in England*, was not
part of a controversy, though it provoked one.
Various attempts were made to answer it, the most
considerable being L'Estrange's.[1] It was reprinted
again and again and became a kind of arsenal for the
anti-government party. The style is clean, sharp and
clear, and uniformly grave. There is an informing
rhythmic power in these sentences describing the
English Government as it should be, a power unknown
to Marvell's earlier prose:

> ...the very meanest Commoner of *England* is repre-
> sented in *Parliament*, and is a party to those Laws by
> which the Prince is sworn to Govern himself and his
> people. No Mony is to be levied but by the common
> consent. No man is for Life, Limb, Goods, or Liberty at
> the Soveraigns discretion: but we have the same Right
> (modestly understood) in our Propriety that the Prince
> hath in his Regality; and in all Cases where the King is
> concerned, we have our just remedy as against any private
> person of the neighbourhood, in the Courts of *Westminster*
> Hall or in the High Court of *Parliament*. His very Pre-
> rogative is no more then what the Law has determined.
> His Broad Seal, which is the Legitimate stamp of his
> pleasure, yet is no longer currant, than upon the Trial it
> is found to be Legal. He cannot commit any person by
> his particular warrant. He cannot himself be witnesse in

---

[1] *An Account of the Growth of Knavery* (1678). He relies almost entirely on scaremongering, in drawing a parallel with 1641. He
distorts Marvell's statements into incitements to rebellion.

any cause: the Ballance of Publick Justice being so dellicate, that not the hand only but even the breath of the Prince would turn the scale. Nothing is left to the Kings will, but all is subjected to his Authority: by which means it follows that he can do no wrong, nor can he receive wrong; and a King of *England*, keeping to these measures, may without arrogance be said to remain the onely Intelligent Ruler over a Rational People.[1]   pp. 3–4.

This positive conception of English rule had been implicit in the satire of the Mock Speech, and directs the scathing analysis of the present work. *The Growth of Popery* divides into four parts. The introduction[2] is a general description of Popery and the Papal influence on government. Marvell does not attack avowed Catholics (whom he praises for suffering disabilities), but the secret supporters of France. The Pope, for Marvell, was in practice not His Holiness, but Louis XIV.

The second part[3] describes the second Dutch War, forced on the country by the French party at Court, and the struggle in Parliament over supplies. The third part[4] is the main body of the work and describes in detail the Parliamentary Session of 1676, the tussle between Charles and Parliament when Parliament demanded a Dutch alliance as the price of voting supplies. The King first tried bullying, then forcibly adjourning the House, which was done three times.

The conclusion[5] briefly urges the seriousness of the situation, the shame and danger to which England is exposed, and protests that the book is not written

[1] Grosart, *Works*, vol. IV, p. 249.
[2] *Ibid.* pp. 248–63.   [3] *Ibid.* pp. 263–319.
[4] *Ibid.* pp. 319–410.   [5] *Ibid.* pp. 411–14.

against the King, but the 'privy conspiracy' of which he and his country are victims.

The situation seemed to Marvell nearly desperate. The backstairs diplomacy—of which the Secret Treaty of Dover is an example—seemed to invalidate any work that was done in the House: the French were ruining trade by privateering in the Channel: and the obvious ally, William of Orange, was neglected if not insulted. Marvell could see no way out of such a situation:

> It is now come to the fourth Act, and the next Scene that opens may be *Rome* or *Paris*, yet men sit by, like idle Spectators, and still give money towards their own *Tragedy*.[1]   p. 155.

The House of Commons itself is so thoroughly corrupt that little is to be hoped from it. Nearly a third of the members were in Charles' service: 'These are all of them indeed to be esteemed Gentlemen of Honor, but more or lesse according to the quality of their severall imployments under his Majesty.'[2] Another third of the members are seeking the same kind of office: 'they are all of them to be bought and sold, only their Number makes them cheaper.'[3] The remaining third are either the best or the worst of men. Some are mere sots:

> But notwithstanding these, there is an hanfull of *Salt*, a sparkle of *Soul*, that hath hitherto preserved this grosse Body from Putrefaction, some *Gentlemen* that are constant, invariable, indeed *English* men, such as are above *hopes*, or *fears*, or *dissimulation*, that can neither flatter, nor betray

---

[1] Grosart, *loc. cit.* p. 412.
[2] *Ibid.* pp. 323-4.   [3] *Ibid.* p. 328.

their King, or Country: But being conscious of their own Loyalty, and Integrity, proceed throw good and bad report, to acquit themselves in their Duty to God, their Prince, and their Nation.[1]   p. 79.

But these few are comparatively helpless against the majority who 'are grown too so familiar among themselves, that...they live together not like Parliament men, but like so many Good-fellows, met together in a Publick House to make merry'.[2]

In this disgraceful situation, when the whole machinery of government was dislocated, and even the venal Commons driven to protest, till 'they were kickt from Adjournment to Adjournment, as from one stair down to another, and when they were at the bottom kickt up again, having no mind yet to *Go out of Doors*':[3] in this situation, Marvell faced things with an unmoved stolidity almost too cool to be called courage. The language is temperate, the matter temperate (as when he praises the avowed Catholics who laid down their offices rather than submit to the Test). He makes no attempt to raise a scare, and his unconscious contribution to the Popish Plot would almost certainly have gone against the grain had he lived to know it:

...the War broke out, and then to be sure Hell's broke loose. Whether it were a War of Religion, or of Liberty, it is not worth the labour to enquire. Which-soever was at the top, the other was at the bottom; but upon considering all, I think the Cause was too good to have been fought for. Men ought to have trusted God; they ought and might have trusted the King with that whole matter....For men may spare their pains where Nature

[2] Grosart, *loc. cit.* p. 329.   [2] *Ibid.* p. 331.   [3] *Ibid.* p. 410.

is at work, and the world will not go the faster for our
driving.[1]   *R.T.* I, p. 303.

The man who wrote thus could not have approved of
the judicial proceedings of his acquaintance Scroggs,
or have failed to see through Titus Oates.

The relief which pamphlets of this kind gave to
popular irritation must have been immense. The
continuous struggle with the King over money matters,
occasional quarrels with the House of Lords, and large
disagreements among themselves made for stormy
sessions in the House of Commons. And whether as a
House of Commons' man of twenty years' standing,
whether as a disciple of Harrington, Marvell certainly
regarded it as the Ruling Instrument; and not only
the Ruling Instrument, but the epitome of the English
people themselves, a sort of national microcosm.
Several of the doubtful pieces attributed to him are
sarcastic notices of the misconduct of various members. The state of Parliament was perhaps the core
of all his exasperation: but the ignominious Dutch
War abroad and the ignominious government at
home were shown up more strongly for one who had,
as he, seen something of government under Cromwell.
There was no encouragement to hope for anything
better under James: but men who did not retreat
to the country found some relief in discussion and
in pamphleteering. Marvell's more immediate and
violent feelings went into his doggerel: the energy
with which he reduces chance victims like Parker
and Turner, in his prose, was not perhaps entirely

[1] Grosart, *Works*, vol. III, p. 212.

provoked by them, but was rather the relief of a deeper and more general disgust. It disappears in *The Growth of Popery*, a plain statement of affairs as they appeared to anxious and experienced people in 1677.

Marvell's letters are lighter reading than his pamphlets: they have a surprising variety of tone, especially the few private letters. (Not that any of them, however private, could be called personal.)

In a letter to William Popple, his nephew, he transcribes the letter from the Bishop of Hereford thanking him for *Mr Smirke* and also his own reply, which opens with a depreciation in the grand manner:

> a good cause receives more injury from a weake defence y^n from a frivolous accusation & ye ill y^t does a man noe harme is to be p^rferred before ye good y^t creates him a p^rjudice. But y^r Ldships generosity is not I see to be reformed by ye most exquisite patterns of ill nature & while perverse men have made a crime of y^r virtue yet 'tis y^r pleasure to convert ye disobligation I have placed upon you into a civility

But he ends with the dangerously pious observation that 'as long as God shall lend you life & health I reckon o^r church is indefectible'.[1]

His power of administering a snub to his constituents when they had informed a certain Mr Cresset of the contents of his confidential despatches is equally dexterous and more pointed:

> ...which makes me presume to advertise you that although I object nothing to Mr Cressets fidelity and discretion neither do I write deliberately any thing which I feare to have divulged yet seeing it is possible that

[1] Margoliouth, *Misc. Letters*, No. 26.

in writing to assured friends a man may give his pen some
liberty and the times are somthing criticall beside that I
am naturally and now more by my Age inclined to keep
my thoughts private, I desire that what I write down to
you may not easily or unnecessarily returne to a third
hand at London.[1]

'I am naturally... inclined to keep my thoughts
private.' But a quality of mind emerges; as in his
verse, Marvell hardly ever speaks merely for himself,
and the effect is neither that of repression nor of incompleteness, but of a spontaneous and quite complete
self-control. His description of the disinterment of
Cromwell may shock by its curt simplicity. When he
was about to start on a journey to Russia and Scandi-
navia with Lord Carlisle's embassy, he wrote a brief
letter to Hull to assure his constituents that their other
member would look after their business, and that he
had had his absence approved by the House so that
there was no need for a by-election:

However I can not but advise also with you desiring to
take your assent along with me... I shall hope to receive
herein your speedy answer.[2]

There was little but a nominal consent left to the
Mayor and burgesses. Marvell seems to have treated
them rather as Charles treated his loyal Commons.

At the same time he was very ready to serve them.
His passion for detail and his conscientious work for
the borough must have been rare in the House at that
time. He writes dozens of letters about a new light-
house, and how to get the best bargains from the
landlord. He is absorbed in questions of duties,

[1] Margoliouth, *Letters to Hull*, No. 197.   [2] *Ibid.* No. 36.

K

Customs dues, and taxation, and writes full despatches whenever the house is sitting. This long series reflects faithfully and dispassionately the events which in his pamphlets he describes in a more personal way, and the contrast is often piquant. The measured tone of the letters (invariably opening 'Gentlemen, my very worthy friends') is something more than polite. In a very early one, Marvell ends:

It is hard for me to write short to you. It seems to me when I have once begun that I am making a step to Hull & can not easily part from so good company.[1]

The aldermen regularly sent him a barrel of ale, which he acknowledged in a high style. And if he were rather peremptory in demanding details of some new project or in asking for money to oil the wheels of government, they seem to have accepted his sharpness with docility. After eighteen years of representation he will unbend so far as to say:

Sir, I must beg your excuse for paper penn writing & every thing. For really I have by ill chance neither eat nor drunke from yesterday at noone till six a clock to night that the house rose and by good chance I have now met with Mr Skyner....[2]

('Mr Skyner' was presumably Cyriack, a friend of his as well as of Milton.)

Now and then he gives a hint of the disappointment with the conduct of affairs which comes out so bitterly in his satires; he says:

God direct all Counsells to the true remedy of the urgent condition of this poore Nation, which I hope there is no reason to despaire of.[3]

[1] Margoliouth, *Letters to Hull*, No. 13. [2] *Ibid.* No. 222. [3] *Ibid.* No. 217.

But even the worst situation can draw little more than:

> But they that discourse the lest and thinke the best of it will be the wisest men and the best Subjects.[1]

The work which Marvell did for the Trinity House at Hull was not always so formally conducted, for his brother-in-law was one of the Brethren. Though even he gets rapped over the knuckles now and then:

> Though your Eys be bad your Understanding is cleare so that I need not advise you to looke unto your side of your businesse.[2]

> Pray who did put you on making distresse whereby you ran your selfe as much as you could into the Common law, whereas this way lay plain before you? I know the Charter impowrs to distrain. But your Charter is not a Magna Charta. Countrey Counsell like ill Tinkers make work for those at London.[3]

But it was of their concerns that Marvell announced:

> I for my part have been put more upon my industry dexterity and courage herein then I have almost in any thing through my whole life.[4]

Before his Russian journey he wrote specially to the Trinity House to say that he had put their affairs into the best hands, and to send the names of those to whom they could apply in case their agents fell sick, assuring them that:

> could I imagine that therein the affairs of your House could receive any detriment, I would absolutely desist from this undertaking.[5]

---

[1] Margoliouth, *Letters to Hull*, No. 279.
[2] Margoliouth, *Trinity House Letters*, No. 47.
[3] *Ibid.* No. 48.
[4] *Ibid.* No. 5.   [5] *Ibid.* No. 8.

K *

In return they sent him not only a yearly barrel of ale as the aldermen did, but also a salmon.

The most interesting group of letters are those to his friends, especially Sir Edward Harley. It is to Sir Edward that he describes Parker's *Reproof* to *The Rehearsal Transpros'd* as 'the rudest book, one or other, that was ever publist (I may say), since the first invention of printing'. But, he continues,

> Although it handles me so roughly yet I am not at all amated by it. But I must desire the advice of some few friends to tell me whether it will be proper for me and in what way to answer it. However I will for mine own private satisfaction forthwith draw up an answer that shall have as much of spirit and solidity in it as my ability will afford & the age we live in will indure.[1]

But in the meantime he wishes the discourse of his friends to suggest that no answer is to be expected to so scurrilous a book, and now 'I intend by the end of the next week to betake my selfe some five miles of to injoy the spring & my privacy'—presumably in his cottage at Highgate.

It is to Sir Edward also that he confides the fortunes of *Mr Smirke*, which was technically anonymous and for the better security of Marvell's ears must remain so, for the comparison of Turner with Mr Smirke of Etherege's *Man of Mode* had involved the comparison of the Duke of York with Sir Fopling Flutter:

> the book said to be Marvels makes what shift it can in the world but the Author walks negligently up & down as unconcerned. The Divines of our Church say it is not in the merry part so good as the Rehearsall Transpros'd, that

[1] Margoliouth, *Misc. Letters*, No. 18.

it runns dreggs: the Essay they confesse is writ well
enough to the purpose he intended it but that was a very
ill purpose. . . . Marvell, if it be he, has much staggerd me
in the busnesse of the Nicene & all Councills, but had
better have taken a rich Presbyterians mony that before
the book came out would have bought the whole Impression to burne it. Who would write? What saith the
poor man.[1]

'The poor man' was the Bishop of Hereford, in whose
diocese Harley lived.

He reports lively conversations of Charles II,
London jests and Scottish jests, the Chandlers' boys'
remedy for the gout, and the king's visit to the latest
new play written against Shaftesbury. He would like
to describe the scene at Shaftesbury's trial, but:

I am afraid to launch into it at the end of a Letter, I am
so subject to be particular. People were at twelve a
clock at night beating up the Hall doore to get in. By
foure in the morning there were no places left. . . Severall
were carryed out of Court for dead. . . .

and so on for half a page or so more.[2]

Marvell had a taste for particular scenes, anecdotes
and the curious, but only when they were part of
public affairs. He enjoys describing how Loads, a
loyal orange merchant, who was proposed as City
Chamberlain, was defeated, and by his adversaries,
'in a malicious City jeere', proposed as Ale-Conner;
but a point was involved which Sir Edward would not
miss. Even Charles' behaviour towards Parliament
was not a sorer point than his attempt to control the
City, and such stories were the easiest way of conveying

---

[1] Margoliouth, *Misc. Letters*, No. 25.   [2] *Ibid.* No. 27.

the strength of feeling on such matters, where direct explanation was virtually impossible: for to be moderately respectful towards the King was only good manners and had nothing to do with politics. It was when he was writing anonymously that Marvell forgot his manners.

The combination of familiarity with well-marked reserves is seen even in his letters to his nephew Will Popple; his expressions are a little stronger perhaps. He can be downright moralistic:

Dr Stubbs physician atheist found dead I meane drowned betwixt Bath & Bristol. 23 guinnies & 3 broad pieces in his pockett suppost drunk. es magne Deus.[1]

To Will also he lets a little of his bitterness escape: 'We are all venal Cowards, except some few',[2] and whereas his account of a monument to Charles I is described to the Hull Corporation as a suitable gesture of loyalty, it is told to Will much in the form of the Satires.[3]

In another letter he almost loses heart: 'In such a Conjuncture, dear *Will*, what Probability is there of my doing any Thing to the Purpose?' But he recovers enough to end with a joke about the situation:

Disce, puer, Virtutem ex me verumque Laborem, Fortunam ex aliis.[4]

Will Popple's rather stiff epitaph for his uncle describes him as

...joining the most peculiar Graces of Wit and Learning/With an singular Penetration and Strength of

---

[1] Margoliouth, *Misc. Letters*, No. 26.
[2] *Ibid.* No. 11.   [3] *Ibid.* No. 23.   [4] *Ibid.* No. 10.

Judgment/And Exercising all these, in the whole Course
of his Life/With an unalterable Steadiness in the Ways of
Virtue/He became the Ornament and Example of his
Age/Beloved by Good Men, feard by Bad, admired by
All,/Though imitated alas by few, and scarse fully
paralleled by any.[1]

One letter by Marvell was published with his poems
in the folio of 1681; and he had presumably kept it
with them. This is the formal letter of consolation
written to Sir John Trott of Laverstoke on the death
of his last surviving son, Edmund, in August 1667. The
Latin epitaph on Edmund Trott was enclosed with it.

Letters of consolation formed almost a distinct
literary *genre*, and Marvell repeats the usual half
a dozen analogies from Scripture: he counsels sub-
mission and fortitude, and then apologizes for seeming
to instruct a man of superior piety; the accent of true
sympathy is reinforced by the impersonality of the
material:

> ...having a great esteem and affection for you, and the
> grateful memory of him that is departed being still green
> and fresh upon my Spirit, I cannot forbear to inquire
> how you have stood the second shock at your sad meeting
> of Friends in the Country....I know the contagion of
> grief, and infection of Tears, and especially when it
> runs in a blood....The Tears of a family may flow
> together like those little drops that compact the Rainbow,
> and if they be plac'd with the same advantage towards
> Heaven as those are to the Sun, they too have their
> splendor: and like that bow while they unbend into
> seasonable showers, yet they promise that there shall not
> be a second flood.[2]

This community of grief, when illustrated by its

---

[1] See p. 15, n. 2.　　[2] Margoliouth, *Misc. Letters*, No. 9.

affinity with natural and beautiful things, should restrain as much as it soothes. Marvell had said the same thing in his poem on *Eyes and Tears*. To indulge the feelings in such a manner must carry with it the guarantee of moderation; and, without danger of appearing insensible, Marvell can point out that while the young man's death is a general loss, the very sense of how generally it is felt should act as reminder that there are calamities which would be greater, because *more* public. When Eli the high priest heard of the death of his two sons:

yet he fell not till the News that the Ark of God was taken. I pray God that we may never have the same paralel perfected in our publick concernments. Then we shall need all the strength of Grace and Nature to support us.

Few men could have better right to urge such an argument than Marvell. Yet a little further on he hesitates, feeling his speech may sound cold:

I could say over upon this beaten occasion most of those lessons of morality and religion that have been so often repeated and are as soon forgotten. We abound with precept, but we want examples.

He is confident that Sir John will provide such an example to the rest of his family; but he does not ignore the cost:

'Tis true, it is an hard task to learn and teach at the same time. And, where your self are the experiment, it is as if a man should dissect his own body and read the Anatomy Lecture. But I will not heighten the difficulty while I advise the attempt.

Sir John's social responsibilities, as well as his piety, make exhortation unnecessary:

I my self, who live to so little purpose, can have little authority or ability to advise you in it, who are a Person that are and may be much more so generally useful.

Modesty, good breeding, sympathy and a sense of social obligations are all blended by Marvell in this sentence.

He does not neglect practical advice: Sir John should look for support in 'The word of God: The society of good men: and the books of the Ancients'; and, in a secondary way, in 'diversion, business, and activity'.

The letter shows very clearly Marvell's power to combine traditional gravity and Restoration elegance. The sentence about the Rainbow might have been written by Jeremy Taylor;[1] but the older school of writers would not have qualified their moralizings, or have had quite Marvell's delicate sense of both the social and individual context. When Donne, for instance, wrote to his mother on the death of his sister, he spoke simply as a priest:

I hope therefore, my most dear Mother, that your experience of the calamities of this life, your continuall acquaintance with the visitations of the holy Ghost, which gives better inward comforts, than the world can outward

[1] Cf. Jeremy Taylor in a passage which Marvell almost certainly heard (*The Golden Grove*, ed. L. Pearsall Smith (Oxford, 1930), p. 78): 'If you do but see a Maiden carried to her grave a little before her intended marriage, or an Infant dye before the birth of Reason, Nature hath taught us to pay a tributary tear....God places a watry cloud in the eye, that when the light of heaven shines upon it, it may produce a rain-bow to be a Sacrament and a memorial that God and the sons of God do not love to see a man perish' (*Sermon preached at the Opening of Parliament*, 1661).

discomforts, your wisdom, to distinguish the value of this world from the next, and your religious fear of offending our mercifull God, by repining at any thing which he doth, will preserve you from any inordinate and dangerous sorrow, for this losse of my most beloved Sister.[1]

When he wrote to Sir Henry Goodyer on the death of his wife, he spoke simply as a friend:

I am almost glad that I knew her so little: for I would have no more additions to sorrow. If I should comfort you, it were an almes acceptable in no other title, than when poor give to poor; for I am more needy of it than you.[2]

With Marvell the personal feeling shows itself only as a fine tact; it does not need direct statement. This, the most formal letter of his that we have, is also the most expressive and the most moving.

The personal correspondence, to sum up, while a shade franker, is not many shades more intimate than the public letters. The courtesy is translated into raillery, the business efficiency into sober moralizing; but they form the same design. This evenness of temper is set off by the violence of the world described; the House in an uproar, 'every Man's Hand on his Hilt', Sir John Coventry with his nose slit by Monmouth's ruffians, Charles sitting laughing in the House of Lords, saying, as the Earl of Clare made to his face a speech against his presence, that it was better than a play. All of which Marvell set down with promptness, exactitude, and equanimity. The total impression is one of a mind so equable and stable that the poems appear to be its natural flowering.

[1] Donne, *Complete Poetry and Selected Prose*, ed. John Hayward (Nonesuch Press, 1930), pp. 472–3.   [2] *Ibid.* p. 447.

APPENDICES

A. MARVELL'S 'MARRIAGE'

The following pages include an account of the dis-
coveries made by Prof. F. S. Tupper, chiefly from legal
records at the Public Record Office. They solve the
question of 'Mary Marvell'; and throw some light on
Marvell's activities during the last year of his life.[1]

In June 1677 the public-spirited Marvell was hiding a
couple of undischarged bankrupts. He took a house in
Great Russell Street, in the name of Mary Palmer, and
here they lay concealed. These men, Edward Nelthorpe
and Richard Thompson, were friends and distant connections of Marvell; both came from Hull.

£500 belonging to these men was deposited with a
goldsmith in Marvell's name. When he died at Great
Russell Street on 16 August 1678, they entered into a
plot with Mary Palmer and John Farringdon, another
of the bankrupts, who was in prison, to recover the
money. Mary Palmer had been Marvell's landlady when
he lodged in Westminster; she was now his housekeeper.
She was an elderly widow of no education and of 'mean
condition' and, for legal purposes, eight months after
Marvell's death she became *his* widow, so that the money
might be claimed by her without the Commissioners of
Bankruptcy being able to seize it.

It was during the long legal tussle that Mary Palmer
found in a little private lodging of Marvell in Maiden
Lane, Covent Garden 'a few Books and papers of a small
value'. Her 'note' to the *Poems* is dated 15 October 1680.
The date of purchase in the Luttrell copy is 18 January
1680/1.

[1] F. S. Tupper, 'Mary Palmer, alias Mrs Andrew Marvell',
P.M.L.A. June 1938 (vol. LIII, No. 2).

But eventually the schemers quarrelled, and Farring-don, who managed the business from the King's Bench Prison, turned against Mary Palmer. He declared that she was not Marvell's widow. She declared she was and even mentioned when and where the marriage had taken place—in May 1667 at Holy Trinity in the Little Minories. The marriage registers for this period are lost; but all the evidence is overwhelmingly against Mary Palmer. Marvell had always treated her simply as a servant. The bankrupts won the money in the end, though not till 1684; but it was never formally established whether the marriage was to be rejected or not. When Mary Palmer died, in 1687, her burial was entered in the register of St Giles-in-the-Fields under her own name, so that she does not seem to have kept up the claim to marriage after she had failed to obtain the money.

In his desire to prove that Marvell could not have left £500, Farringdon said that he was practically penniless; that for five years before he died he had not been worth £100, and that his whole estate at his death was not worth £30. It was to Farringdon's interest to say so, of course; and everyone connected with the case seems to have committed perjury without scruple. Farringdon also said that Marvell had for several years been supported at intervals by his firm, which was connected with the wine business of Marvell's nephew, Will Popple.[1]

Both parties stressed Marvell's learning and his Parliamentary reputation; Farringdon mentioned it as a reason why he would have been unlikely to marry 'so mean a person' as Mary Palmer; and Mrs Palmer mentioned it as being the reason for his keeping the marriage secret. Mrs Palmer could hardly be dismissed on the evidence of Farringdon; her own conduct is the strongest proof that she was not Marvell's wife. She made no claims till eight months after his death; she could not remember exactly when he died; and dropped her title

---

[1] But cf. Marvell's only reference to money to Will, 'Ignoscas Gulielme curiositati meae...' (Margoliouth, *Misc. Letters*, No. 26). Here Will seems to be the poorer of the two.

to his name without any external pressure when the case
was over. One may add to these facts the impression
given by the depositions of Mary Palmer; which, if to
any degree they represent her own speech, behind that
of the lawyer who compiled them for her, show her as a
garrulous and small-minded woman:

And though it be true likewise That the said Andrew Marvell
was a Parliam^t man and a Learned man Yet it doth not follow
but that he might marry this Defend^t as in truth he did...she
did what she could to conceal the same And therefore she did
sometimes attend on him more like a Servant than Wife
(Which was the better to conceal their being man and wife)
And whilest the said Mr Nelthorp and this Defend's husband
dwelt together in the house aforesaid True it is she did not
always sit down with them at Meales having sometimes other
Occasions But she did very often and so often as she pleased set
down with them at Meales and Eat her Meat with them.

The deception was at first contrived for Mary Palmer by
the bankrupts; when she had to sustain it against them,
she must have felt rather as Mrs Bardell would have
done if Messrs Dodson and Fogg had suddenly become
attorneys for the defendant.

The whole case is very squalid, and to an age in which
the law is no longer such a quag of delays and injustice
it probably appears more criminal than it did to contemporaries. Marvell's part in the affair was to shelter
the two men who were in danger of prison, and to deposit
some of their money in his name. Whether he did this out
of old friendship or because of pecuniary obligation or
because of political sympathy, it did not involve him in
active fraud and perjury. Farringdon accused him of
being responsible for a Bill in Parliament which decreed
special penalties against the members of the firm because
they had destroyed their books and otherwise hindered
the work of the Commissioners of Bankruptcy; but there
is no evidence that Marvell had any hand in promoting
the Bill, and the suggestion that he was planning the
death of the men he sheltered is absurd as well as re-
volting. His reference to this Private Bill in his letter to

L

the Hull Corporation of 12 February 1677/8 is very brief;
but some of the Corporation would certainly know that
he was actually hiding the fugitives!

Had it not been for this slightly disreputable action of
Marvell, it is very unlikely that any of the poems for
which he is read to-day would have been given to the
world. When they appeared they were no longer in
fashion, and the volume seems to have sold chiefly as a
memorial to Marvell the patriot; in most copies the
portrait is missing as though it had been taken out to
frame. Perhaps readers hoped to find in the volume some
of those dangerous anonymous satires on which Marvell's
reputation was based in his lifetime; *they* were in the
height of fashion, and would have been much appreciated
by the Opposition, but none of them were included. It
was perhaps thought too dangerous to print them; the
printer would certainly have been in danger, and since he
excised even the political poetry of the Commonwealth
period, he must have been a prudent man. They appeared
separately in collections, however, with Marvell's name
attached; and his name was put on the title page of the
second edition of *The Growth of Popery*, which came out in
the year of his death.

The lyrical poems sold on the reputation of their
author and not because they were to the taste of the time;
perhaps the publisher reckoned on this, for Mary
Palmer sounds as if she were as 'unpoetical' as Shakespeare's Audrey. The fact that the 'inconsolable widow'
gave such things as *The Definition of Love* and *To his Coy
Mistress* to the public (not to mention the improprieties
of *Daphnis and Chloe* or *Ametas and Thestylis*) is not a legal
point against Mary Palmer, but it is calculated to make
the critic more grateful than ever for her stupidities while
sceptical of her pretensions.

B. MARVELL'S JOURNEY TO RUSSIA

A Relation/of Three/Embassies/From his Sacred *Majestie*/Charles II/To the/Great Duke of Muscovie,/ The King of Sweden, and/The King of Denmark./*Performed by the Right Honble the/Earle of Carlisle*/in the Years 1663 & 1664./Written by an Attendant on the Embassies,/and published with his L^{ps} Approbation./*London,*/Printed for *John Starkey* at the *Miter* in *Fleet-/street* near *Temple-Barr. 1669.* [By G. Miège.]

The Arrival

P. 23....he arrived the 19. of *August* at the Barr of *Archangel*, which was seventeen daies before us. And there it was his Frigat came first to an anchor, in expectation of Orders for his Entry, for which reason he sent Mr. *Marvel* his Secretary into the Town. Of whose landing, the Governour having notice, ordered him to be conducted by six Gentlemen to the Castle, through a Regiment of six hundred men, and the next day he sent sixteen boats, guarded by several hundreds of men, under the command of a Collonel, to receive his Excellence, and bring him ashore.

Russian Sports

P. 55. They have also publique Engins to Swing withal, like a double gallowes, having four places for four men, all in an equal distance, where having placed themselves, they swing continually by the Counterpoise they give one another, so that while some swing up to the heighth of a Wind-mill, one may see the others falling near as low as the Ground: which they do successively, till they think it fit to hold. The Women have Ropes which they swing with, or else they lay a plank cross a block, and mounting one at one end, and the other at the other, they toss themselves up with a very violent motion.

Travelling Costumes

P. 93. Insomuch that in a short time we were all in our Robes, some like *Muscovites*, others like the *Samojedes*, and some of them in their Sheep-skin Vests with long sleeves, resembling those old and eternal Destinies, whom *Venus* did so laugh at when she saw them in their habits, those like the *Samojedes* looking so hideously that we made a good sport with them.

English Sports

P. 99. And indeed the Musique was very good, being managed by one of the best experienced Musicians of *England*, who from time to time composed new aires.... But they that knew how to march upon their Scates, did also divert themselves with sliding upon the River. [On the fifth of November] We began our Solemnity in the night by artificial fire-works, made by an *Englishman* with great skill and success; and the same was continued by a great Feast which the *English* Merchants were invited to, and by a pleasant farce of Mascarads after Supper, and concluded with dancing.

Russian Smokers

P. 101. Although Tobacco be forbidden in this Country with great severity, yet there were some of the Ambassadors Servants who drove a private Trade with it in this Town, and that with so much advantage, that sometimes they sold the most ordinarie tobacco (which cost them in *London* not above nine pence or ten pence the pound) for fifteen shillings the pound to the *Muscovites*, who stole to them with great secrecy to buy it.... Instead of Pipes they have an Engine made of a Cows horn, in the middle of which they pierce a hole and therein place the Vessel which holds their tobacco. The Vessel is commonly made of wood, very wide and indifferently deep, which when they have filled with tobacco, they put water into the horn to temper the smoak; then they lighten their pipe with a firebrand, and suck the smoak thorough the horn with such greediness, that they make not above two sucks of a pipe; and when they whiffe it out of their mouths, they raise such a cloud that it hides all their face; and immediatly after they fall drunk upon the ground. Five or six of them one after another have I seen tumbling in this manner, and so drunk that they had scarce time to give their Companions their pipes, and for half a quarter of an hour they will ly in this pickle as insensible as if they had the falling sickness. But assoon as they begin to revive, and the smoak of the tobacco hath had its operation, they leap up in an instant one after another more brisk and lively than they were before, pronouncing it a most admirable invention for purging the head.

Marvell snubs an Official, who ripostes

[On being refused sledges for transport] P. 105....my Lord Ambassador dispatched his Secretary to him, who told him freely it was most undecent to have persons of quality worse accommodated for their confidence in the Care of the *Tzar* so great a Monarch, than if they had been at their own charges. He replied they might do as they pleased, no body hindered them from takeing their own course. And thereupon he declared that his Excellence had no reason, to complain, that his *Tzarskoy* Majesty had done him extraordinary honor in sending a person of his quality so far to conduct him to *Mosco*. To which the Secretary replied, that my Lord Ambassador acknowledged his quality, but that he never thought it so great, that he and his associate ought to preferr themselves before him as they had done at their first visit.

[After a dispute whether Carlisle or the Tzar's messenger should alight from the sledges first, it was agreed they should get out together.] P. 132. But in this *Pronchissof* tooke occasion to deceive his Excellence, and falsify his word, hanging in the aire betwixt the armes of his servants, and but touching the earth with his tiptoes, whilst the Ambassador came out freely.

Marvell enters Moscow

[In the grand procession to the Kremlin.] P. 146. In the Ambassadors sledg there was the Secretary and the chief Interpreter standing and uncovered, the Secretarie carrying in his hands upon a yard of red Damaske his Letters of Credence written in parchment, whose Superscription contained all the titles of the *Tzar* in letters of Gold.

Delivers the Ambassador's Address in Latin.

Pp. 177–8. Those two Shafts of the Imperial Quiver, which at what so ever glorious marke Your Majestie shall draw them you can miss with neither: Those two Pledges of peace to Your Subjects and a double terrour to your Enemies... Certainly augurating that those two Sonnes of the *Russian* Eagle, as they are now sharpning their sight daily at the most clear eyes of Your Imperial Majestie, so will also in due time extend their wings after Your example, and soar to the highest pitch that true virtue and indefatigable labour can carry the magnanimous offspring of Princes.

Marvell is misunderstood

[This speech was disliked, because the Tzar was addressed as *Illustrissimus*: he preferred *Serenissimus* and there were several diplomatic exchanges over this point. A much worse misinterpretation of Marvell's Latin happened after they had started home. Carlisle had petitioned for one Calthrop to return with him, his term of service with the Tzar being up. This was allowed, but after they had gone some way a messenger appeared, apprehended Calthrop and took him back to Moscow where he was imprisoned. Carlisle wrote protesting and demanding Calthrop's liberty, but] Pp. 318–19. This Letter was so farr from making any favourable impressions in the *Tzar*, that it exasperated him to that heighth, he resolved immediately to dispatch an Ambassador to the

King of *England* to complain of his Excellences proceedings. The design was principally taken upon a pleasant
mistake on their side, of *qui* for *quid.* For this Expression
in the Letter, *Quorum haec vergant nescio, neque vos ipsi scitis
qui facitis* which signifyes as it is translated, how farr these
things may extend I know not, nor You Your selves who
contrive them, the Court of *Muscovie* mis-interpreted it
thus, *I know not what may be the end of this busines, nor do You
know Your selves what You do.*

A Delicate Compliment that became too Obvious

[In Sweden.] Pp. 373–4. Whilst the Ambassador was
making this Complement [to the Queen] there happened
an accident that surprised all the Company. For about
the middle of his Speech where he saith, *That the
boldest Eloquence would lose its Speech*, his Excellence
made a long pause, as if by that he had designed to
have verified what he had said. For my part at first
I believed it was the sincerity of my Lord Ambassadors discourse that produced this effect, and that
it being too great a task for him to represent to the
Queen, the great honour his Master the King of *England*
had for her, and the great sence himself had of the
Favours which he had received from her Majesty, his
Speech had failed him.... But when I saw the Secretary
fall himself upon the same rock, and stop in the same
place when he interpreted the Complement in *French*,
then I concluded the thing had been so contrived. At
length both of them having recollected, they finished the
Harangue...

More Sports

P. 378. The principal divertisement we received all this
Voiage was given us by a couple of tame Bears, which we
brought with us from *Mosco.* One of them was so gentle,
that one might beat him or play with him as with a Spaniel,
for he managed his teeth and his claws with that careful-
ness and dexterity, that he never did anybody hurt. And
having been taught to wrestle, he in a short time attained

to perfection in it, and took great delight in that recreation. The other that was something the bigger of the two was of another humour and quality, his pleasure was to suck peoples fingers, insomuch that to endear ones self to him, there was no more to be done but to put ones finger into his mouth (which was very often done) and suffer him to suck it, as if it were a Teat. Sometimes he would bite a little, or give a pat with his foot if one passed by upon the Deck without treating him in that manner.

Marvell starts a Free Fight

[Quarrel near Hamburg.] Pp. 430–1. For being upon the point of departing after dinner, and having hired fresh waggons to make three or four leagues that night, it hapned that the Secretaries wagoner would not stir, unless there might go along with him another wagoner his Comrade, who would have been as useless to us as his waggon. The Secretary not able to bring him to reason by fair means, tried what he could do by foul, and by clapping a pistol to his head would have forced him along with him. But immediately his pistol was wrested from him, and as they were putting themselves into a posture to abuse him, we interposed so effectually, that he was rescued out of the hands of a barbarous rout of peasants and Mechanicks. But whilst the Secretary was going to the Governour to desire him to take some order in the case, we found the rest of us beset by above a hundred of them... [They lost some firearms, a little Spaniel, and a page lost his Periwig in the combat, and wearing a Samojede cap underneath looked 'so unlike a Christian' that he was tossed in the snow by the mob. 'His Excellence' who had started out, returned with the alarum of the skirmish, and eventually they got off with four waggons instead of five.]

C. MARVELL AND SPINOZA

The possibility of Marvell having read Spinoza is not remote, though there is nothing which could lead to anything stronger than speculation and conjecture.

Spinoza was known in England. His most constant correspondent, Henry Oldenburg (to whom he wrote regularly between 1661 and 1667), was the Secretary of the Royal Society and also a personal friend of Milton. Marvell could have met Oldenburg at Milton's house. Spinoza's reputation as an 'atheist' provoked the clergy of the Church of England: in the Cambridge University Library there are no less than five refutations of Spinoza, all written before 1688, and all by churchmen.

Marvell knew Holland well, as his early poem *The Character of Holland* proves. He visited the country on his first foreign tour in 1640–4. At this time Spinoza was a boy, but on the occasion of Marvell's second visit (June 1662–April 1663) he was already famous. He had been excommunicated in 1656: he was living at Rhijnsberg between 1660 and 1663: his 'club' of followers in Amsterdam were spreading his theories and for them he was actually writing the *Ethics* at this time, having already composed the *Short Treatise on God, Man and Well-Being*.

Marvell would have an introduction to the academic circles of Holland through his intimate 'acquaintance' John Pell, who had been Professor of Mathematics at Amsterdam 1643–6 and at Breda 1646–52. He would have a larger general acquaintance through the large number of Puritan exiles who went to Holland at the Restoration. Amsterdam had become a byword in England as a centre of disaffection. The *Letter from Amsterdam* which gives a satiric notice of Marvell (see Chapter 1, p. 8, n. 1) was really a London production. Marvell's own *Growth of Popery* was stated on the title page of the first edition (published in his life-time) to have been 'printed at Amsterdam'; but this may not be true, for dangerous books were often stated to have been printed abroad in order to help in concealing the printer.

Richard Baxter's translation of Chapter xvi of Spinoza's *Tractatio Theologico-Politicus* (1670) was made and printed, though not published, by 1676. It appeared in Chapter vi of the Second Part of *The Nonconformist's Plea for Peace* (1680) which gives '*The marrow of Spinoza's Opera posthuma which I read not till after the writing of what is before. To which Hobbes much agreeth*' (pp. 107–16.) See F. J. Powicke, *The Reverend Richard Baxter under the Cross*, 1662–1691 (Jonathan Cape, 1927), pp. 188–98.

John Howe's Animadversions on Spinoza in Chapter i of *The Living Temple*, Part II, 'Wherein is shown the destructiveness of Spinoza's scheme and design to religion and the temple of God...', appeared in 1702. See Frederick Pollock, *Spinoza, His Life and Philosophy* (Kegan Paul, 1880), pp. 383–4.

As Marvell had been taunted for his knowledge of Baxter's *A Holy Commonwealth* (see p. 21), and in *The Rehearsal Transpros'd* had defended him, Baxter's interest in Spinoza is of especial importance in this connection. Howe's consideration of the *Ethics* is not so immediately to the point, since it was probably not written till after Marvell's death.

The connection between the doctrine of Spinoza and the writings of Marvell consists rather in a certain general similarity than in any specific parallels. Some of these general likenesses have been mentioned in the text. The most striking are Marvell's elevation of matter to a position equal to that of mind (e.g. in *A Dialogue between the Soul and Body*) and Spinoza's twin attributes of thought and extension (*Ethics*, ii, Props 1–4, 7; v, 1; v, 21, 32 c). This is a feature of his philosophy which most strongly differentiates it from that of his contemporaries. Marvell's three stages of knowledge, as shown in *To his Coy Mistress*, recall Spinoza's three states of knowledge (*Ethics*, ii, 40, Note 2 *et sqq.*), and Marvell's treatment of the passions in this poem and in *The Definition of Love* suggest Spinoza's theory that the passions cease to be passions as soon as we form a clear and distinct idea of them (*Ethics*, v, 2, 3).

INDEX

NOTE: *the most important references are given in*
heavy type

A. GENERAL INDEX

B. MARVELL AND HIS WORKS

www.ingramcontent.com/pod-product-compliance
Ingram Content Group UK Ltd.
Pitfield, Milton Keynes, MK11 3LW, UK
UKHW042144280225
455719UK00001B/94